First Workshop on Evaluations and Assessments of Neural Conversation Systems (EANCS 2021)

Online
11 November 2021

ISBN: 978-1-7138-9186-4

Printed from e-media with permission by:

Curran Associates, Inc.
57 Morehouse Lane
Red Hook, NY 12571

Some format issues inherent in the e-media version may also appear in this print version.

Printed with permission by Curran Associates, Inc. (2024)

For permission requests, please contact the Association for Computational Linguistics at the address below.

Association for Computational Linguistics
209 N. Eighth Street
Stroudsburg, Pennsylvania 18360

Phone: 1-570-476-8006
Fax: 1-570-476-0860

acl@aclweb.org

Additional copies of this publication are available from:

Curran Associates, Inc.
57 Morehouse Lane
Red Hook, NY 12571 USA
Phone: 845-758-0400
Fax: 845-758-2633
Email: curran@proceedings.com
Web: www.proceedings.com

EANCS 2021

The First Workshop on Evaluations and Assessments of Neural Conversation Systems

Proceedings of the Workshop

Nov 11, 2021
Online

Introduction

Much progress has been made recently to improve conversation systems and chatbots using neural based deep models. While the architectures of conversation models evolve quickly, evaluation techniques over the years remain unchanged. As a matter of fact, evaluating and assessing conversation models has been a decades long challenge. One part of the difficulty comes from the fact that human dialogues exist in a variety of forms. Existing approaches that compare generated conversations from a neural model with ground truth can easily incur large biases due to the lack of diversity. Another part of the difficulty comes from the interactive nature of conversations, which often requires an agent (usually a real person), to conduct the assessments. Human evaluations, on the other hand, can introduce a large amount of variance and are often impractical on a large scale. A third dimension of evaluation has to do with the fairness and reliability of the models, which has become an increasingly important issue for commercial use of neural based systems. Finally, transferability, transparency and ethical issues in evaluations are among some of the other important topics to explore.

Organizing Committee

Wei Wei, Google Cloud AI Research
Bo Dai, Google Brain
Tuo Zhao, Georgia Institute of Technology
Lihong Li, Amazon
Diyi Yang, Georgia Institute of Technology
Yun-Nung Chen, National Taiwan University
Y-Lan Boureau, Facebook AI Research
Asli Celikyilmaz, Microsoft Research
Alborz Geramifard, Facebook AI Research
Aman Ahuja, Virginia Tech University
Haoming Jiang, Amazon Search

Table of Contents

Conference Program

Counterfactual Matters: Intrinsic Probing For Dialogue State Tracking
Yi Huang, Junlan Feng, Xiaoting Wu and Xiaoyu Du

GCDF1: A Goal- and Context- Driven F-Score for Evaluating User Models
Alexandru Coca, Bo-Hsiang Tseng and Bill Byrne

Unsupervised Testing of NLU models with Multiple Views
Radhika Arava, Matthew Trager, Boya Yu and Mohamed Abdelhady

A Comprehensive Assessment of Dialog Evaluation Metrics
Yi-Ting Yeh, Maxine Eskenazi and Shikib Mehri

User Response and Sentiment Prediction for Automatic Dialogue Evaluation
Sarik Ghazarian, Behnam Hedayatnia, Alexandros Papangelis, Yang Liu and Dilek Hakkani-Tur

SERI: Generative Chatbot Framework for Cybergrooming Prevention
Pei Wang, Zhen Guo, Lifu Huang and Jin-Hee Cho

Counterfactual Matters: Intrinsic Probing For Dialogue State Tracking

Yi Huang, Junlan Feng*, Xiaoting Wu, Xiaoyu Du
JIUTIAN Team, China Mobile Research
{huangyi, fengjunlan, wuxiaoting, duxiaoyu}@chinamobile.com

Abstract

A Dialogue State Tracker (DST) is a core component of modular task-oriented dialogue systems. Tremendous research progress has been made in past ten years to improve performance of DSTs especially on benchmark datasets. However, their generalization to novel and realistic scenarios beyond the held-out conversations is limited. In this paper, we design experimental studies to answer: 1) How does the distribution of dialogue data affect the performance of DSTs? 2) What are effective ways to probe counterfactual matter for DSTs? Our findings are: the performance variance of generative DSTs is not only due to the model structure itself, but can be attributed to the distribution of cross-domain values. Evaluating iconic generative DST models on MultiWOZ dataset with counterfactuals results in a significant performance drop of up to 34.64% (from 50.91% to 16.27%) in absolute joint goal accuracy. It is believed that our experimental results can guide the future work to better understand the intrinsic core of DST and rethink the suitable way for specific tasks given the application property.

1 Introduction

A dialogue state tracker (DST) is a pillar of today's task-oriented dialogue systems, which maintains user's intentional goals through the course of a dialogue.

In recent years, the creation of large-scale datasets, such as MultiWOZ (Budzianowski et al., 2018), has fueled the advance of DST models, pushing the accuracy of DST from 15.8%, baseline from (Budzianowski et al., 2018) to above 50% (Lee et al., 2019; Eric et al., 2020; Chen et al., 2020; Goel et al., 2019; Gao et al., 2019; Wu et al., 2019; Zhang et al., 2019; Huang et al., 2020). The common belief is that the more abundant the labeled data, the higher the likelihood of learning diverse phenomena, which in turn leads to models that generalize well. In practice, however, generalization remains as a huge challenge (Yogatama et al., 2019; Linzen, 2020).

Motivated by this phenomenon, we aim to address and provide insights into the following question: how well do DST models generalize to the novel but realistic scenarios that are not captured well enough by the held-out evaluation set? Answering this question may take us a step closer to bridging the gap between dataset collection and broader task objectives (Li et al., 2020; Heck et al., 2020).

Most prior work (Iyyer et al., 2018; Jin et al., 2020) focus on adversarial example generation for robustness evaluation. They rely on perturbations made directly on test examples in the held-out set and assume direct access to evaluated models' gradients or outputs, which often leads to unnatural examples or hurt target models deliberately. Our studies in this paper are not this line of research.

Recently, the generation-model based approaches for DST instead of a close-set classification approach have attracted more attention. Wu proposed a TRAnsferable Dialogue statE generator (TRADE) (Wu et al., 2019) that generates dialogue states from utterances using a copy mechanism, facilitating knowledge transfer between domains. The prominent difference from previous one-domain DST models is that TRADE is based on a generation approach instead of a close-set classification approach. Huang proposed a Meta-Reinforced Multi-Domain State Generator (MERET) (Huang et al., 2020) which introduces an end-to-end generative framework with pretrained language model and copy-mechanism, using RL-based generator to encourage higher semantic relevance in greater exploration space for DST. MERET holds the similar underlying architecture with TRADE. Quan released Modeling Long Context for Task-Oriented Dialogue State Generation

*Corresponding author.

Proceedings of the First Workshop on Evaluations and Assessments of Neural Conversation Systems, pages 1–6
Nov 11, 2021. ©2021 Association for Computational Linguistics

(LCDSG) (Quan and Xiong, 2020), which is a multi-task learning model with a simple yet effective utterance tagging technique and a bidirectional language model as an auxiliary task for task-oriented dialogue state generation. LCDSG follows the similar overall framework with TRADE, too.

We conduct our studies in this paper on top of these models TRADE, MERET and LCDSG: first, we propose a simple and efficient counterfactual-maker policy as a principled approach to generate novel scenarios; then, we take a closer look at data sets, and conduct a deep qualitative analysis on data distribution and model structure impact for the DSTs. The main contributions of this paper are two-fold:

- This paper provides deep analysis of counterfactual probing to mainstream generative DST models.
- This paper empirically examines the performance degradation of generative DSTs at different granularities.

2 Proposed Approach: SVS

Let us define $D = \{(U_1, R_1), ..., (U_T, R_T)\}$ as the set of user utterance and system response pairs in T turns of a dialogue, and $B = \{B_1, ..., B_T\}$ as the dialogue state for each turn. Dialogue state is represented as slot-value pairs, denoted as $B_t = \{(S_1, V_1), ..., (S_J, V_J)\}$ where S_j and V_j $(1 \leq j \leq J)$ denote the j-th slot name and slot value at this turn.

We propose a simple counterfactual-maker approach, Slot Value Substitution (SVS). It is used to generate counterfactual dialogue D' and corresponding dialogue state B'. Parameter m is used to represent the ratio of SVS. For each dialogue, m percent slot values in B_T are selected to be substituted. Specifically, for each slot value V_j, if the value does not appear in dialogue history, we keep it as it is. For values that can be substituted, new values are sampled from ontology, a predefined value set for each domain-slot. Then dialogue history is updated by these new values and counterfactual dialogue D' is generated. For state of each previous turn, B_t $(1 \leq t \leq T)$ is updated and denoted as B'_t. We get $B' = \{(S_1, V'_1), ..., (S_J, V'_J)\}$ for D' after the update and we do post-processing human validation on the counterfactuals generated by SVS to ensure quality. An example of SVS process is shown in Figure 1.

3 Experiments and analysis

In this section, we first describe our observations and concerns from the experiments and then investigate the reason behind.

To evaluate the DSTs' performance on counterfactual dialogue data, we train DST models following their publicly released implementations on the standard train/dev/test split of MultiWOZ[1] from scratch. Joint goal accuracy is used to be the evaluation metric. It measures the accuracy of model prediction at each dialogue turn, and the output is considered correct if and only if all the predicted values exactly match the ground truth values.

3.1 Behavioral probe : Characterization

We compare joint goal accuracy of TRADE, MERET and LCDSG on counterfactuals generated by SVS with different m. Experimental results are listed in Table 1. Surprisingly with m increasing, joint goal accuracy of each model significantly drops, up to 34.64% when m=100. This behavior makes us very curious about the causes behind. We probe the reasons from the perspective of data distribution, characterizing data instances.

Figure 2 shows an overview of error rate of fifteen domain-slots on three test sets. The error rate of most slots increases as m increases, and *train-departure* increases the most, from 2.55% to 20.69%.

To further understand the deep-dive reasons, we conduct qualitative analysis on the data generated by SVS in the next. Figure 3 shows the slot value distribution of *train-departure*, with left vertical axis referring to the proportion of data sets. Through the visual display, we can see the variance between training and test sets with different m clearly: for example, the slot value *cambridge* gets a proportion drop of 0.431 on test set (0.468 vs. 0.037). The data distribution between training and test sets matches well when m=0, while significantly differs when m=100. More generally, the increase of m exacerbates this difference. Extreme situation goes for those unseen slot values appearing in the new test set when m=100. This illustrates the qualitative distribution in-depth, that is, out-of-distribution (OOD) resulting in performance drop of DSTs responding to above.

We also calculate overall F1 on *train-departure* in Figure 3, with right vertical axis representing

[1] https://www.repository.cam.ac.uk/handle/1810/280608

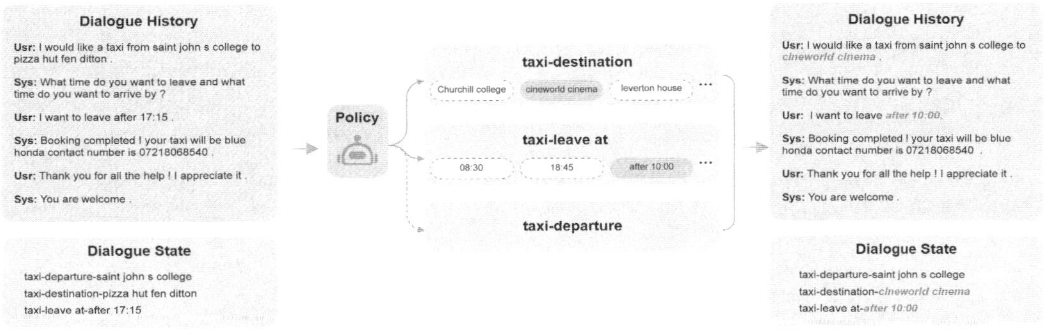

Figure 1: The process of SVS. The left is a dialogue example and the dialogue-level belief state. Value candidates for every checked slot will be substituted by a policy. The right is the substituted dialogue and belief states with new slot values.

DST Model	Joint goal accuracy m=0	m=10	m=20	m=30	m=50	m=80	m=90	m=100
TRADE	0.4913	0.4585	0.3826	0.3290	0.2595	0.1907	0.1768	0.1553
MERET	0.5091	0.4769	0.3977	0.3442	0.2686	0.2039	0.1855	0.1627
LCDSG	0.5103	0.4777	0.4084	0.3557	0.2819	0.2112	0.2032	0.1759

Table 1: Joint goal accuracy of MultiWOZ held-out set with different proportion of slot value substitution. As the proportion of SVS increases, the accuracy drops significantly.

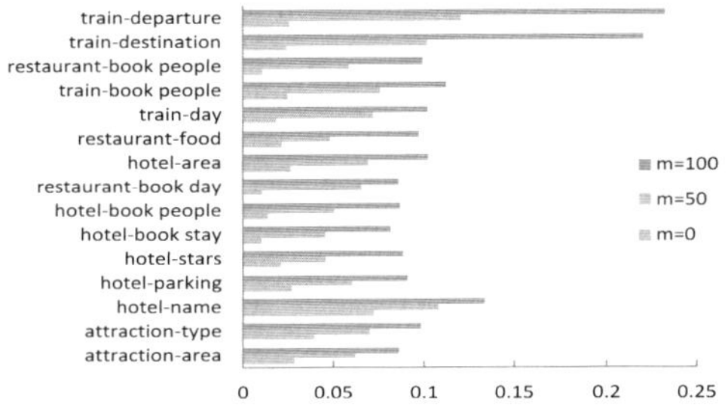

Figure 2: Error rate of multi-domain slots on three test sets. As the ratio of SVS increases, the error rate of *train-departure* and *train-destination* increase by 18.14% and 17.23%.

the results of F1. It shows that for every single slot value, F1 is strongly influenced by the data distribution consistency between training and test sets. The F1 is relatively high when the distribution is consistent. It decreases when m increases. Take *cambridge* for example, 0.956 vs. 0.321 for m=0 and m=100, respectively.

3.2 Structural probe: Attention

In the following, we take TRADE as a representative here, considering the similar structure beings. TRADE consists of two parts in general: a classifier and a copy-mechanism. Copy-mechanism utilizes the generative composition to realize copy action. Detailed experimental results in Table 2 show that the classifier maintains a high accuracy under different conditions. Hence, in the following we focus on analyzing the impact to the second part, the generative composition.

First, we calculate the accuracy of generative composition in counterfactuals generated by SVS with different m. Table 2 is the accuracy of generative composition which shows that as the ratio of SVS increases, the accuracy of generative composition gradually decreases, indicating that the network structure of generative composition is not robust when the ratio of SVS increases.

We reason that counterfactual probing leads to two fundamental changes: the final output distribution and the underlying attention change in different test set. Technically, the final output distribution is:

$$p_{jk}^{f} = p_{jk}^{gen} \times P_{jk}^{v} + (1 - p_{jk}^{gen}) \times P_{jk}^{h} \quad (1)$$

At decoding step k for the j-th (domain, slot) pair, p_{jk}^{f} is final output distribution. P_{jk}^{h} is the probability of the dialogue and P_{jk}^{v} is the probability of the vocabulary, both of them are impacted by attention. The scalar p_{jk}^{gen} is trainable to combine this two distributions. Figure 4 shows p_{jk}^{gen} rises

Compositions	Accuracy of different m							
	m=0	m=10	m=20	m=30	m=50	m=80	m=90	m=100
Generative composition	0.8949	0.8737	0.8313	0.7932	0.7263	0.6265	0.6015	0.5679
Classifier composition	0.9761	0.9758	0.9746	0.9737	0.9722	0.9700	0.9692	0.9681

Table 2: The accuracy of the generative composition and classifier composition under different ratio of SVS. With m increasing, the accuracy drops from 89.94% to 56.79% in generative composition.

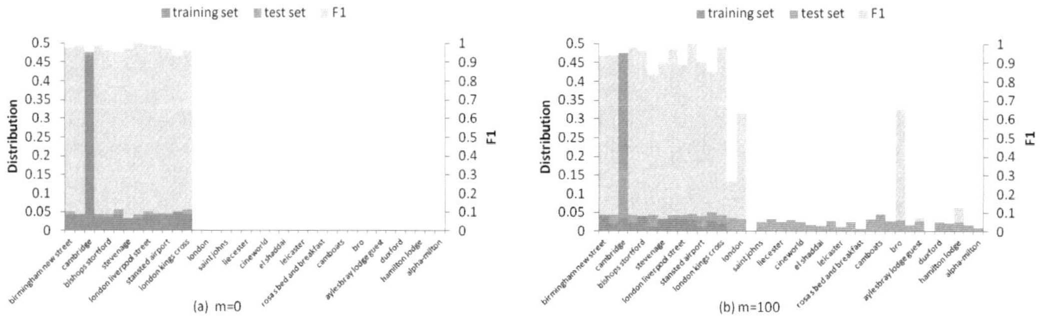

Figure 3: Qualitative analysis for the slot value distribution of *train-departure*. Best viewed in color.

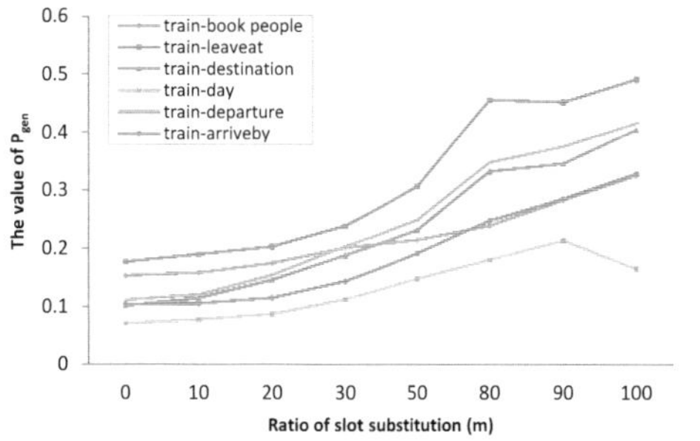

Figure 4: The trend of p_{jk}^{gen} in the *train* domain on different ratio of SVS.

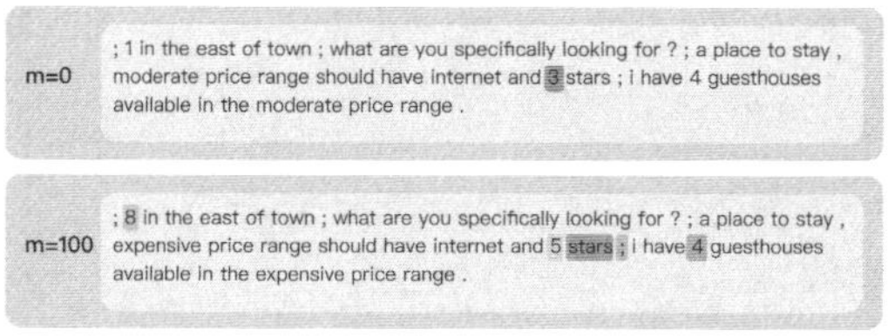

Figure 5: In the dialogue PMUL2513.json, the distribution of attention changes in *hotel-stars* when m differs.

with the increase of SVS ratio in the *train* domain.

It can be seen when the ratio of SVS increases, the model tends to generate from the vocabulary rather than the dialogue. Intuitively, this is one of the reasons for the decline of joint goal accuracy. More unseen values mean larger problem space, existing DST model is insensitive to the unseen test data, which oughts to make the model more inclined to choose the slot value in the dialogue to improve the situation going forward.

To further evaluate the attention matter, we decompose the attention tensor apart from the model structure. Figures 5 shows the distribution of attention in the dialogue when TRADE generates slot values in *hotel-stars*, where darker blue shades indicate larger attention weights. It reveals that the increase of SVS ratio will affect the attention, and then affect the results of generative composition.

4 Conclusions

This paper analyzes reasons leading to performance degradation of generative DSTs across controllable counterfactuals. We propose a simple and efficient counterfactual-maker policy as a principled approach to generate novel scenarios beyond the held-out conversations. We find that performance degradation of DSTs comes from the OOD of counterfactuals and generative composition. These findings are confirmed through experiments on behavior and structure probing, with similar trends. This is of practical interest for applications of DST models, with respect to unlock a true potential of generalization capability.

Acknowledgements

This work is supported by the National Key R&D Program of China under Grant No. 2020AAA0108600.

References

Pawel Budzianowski, Tsung-Hsien Wen, Bo-Hsiang Tseng, Iñigo Casanueva, Stefan Ultes, Osman Ramadan, and Milica Gasic. 2018. Multiwoz - A large-scale multi-domain wizard-of-oz dataset for task-oriented dialogue modelling. In *Proceedings of the 2018 Conference on Empirical Methods in Natural Language Processing, Brussels, Belgium, October 31 - November 4, 2018*, pages 5016–5026.

Lu Chen, Boer Lv, Chi Wang, Su Zhu, Bowen Tan, and Kai Yu. 2020. Schema-guided multi-domain dialogue state tracking with graph attention neural networks. In *The Thirty-Fourth AAAI Conference on Artificial Intelligence, AAAI 2020, The Thirty-Second Innovative Applications of Artificial Intelligence Conference, IAAI 2020, The Tenth AAAI Symposium on Educational Advances in Artificial Intelligence, EAAI 2020, New York, NY, USA, February 7-12, 2020*, pages 7521–7528.

Mihail Eric, Rahul Goel, Shachi Paul, Abhishek Sethi, Sanchit Agarwal, Shuyang Gao, Adarsh Kumar, Anuj Goyal, Peter Ku, and Dilek Hakkani-Tur. 2020. MultiWOZ 2.1: A consolidated multi-domain dialogue dataset with state corrections and state tracking baselines. In *Proceedings of the 12th Language Resources and Evaluation Conference*, pages 422–428, Marseille, France. European Language Resources Association.

Shuyang Gao, Abhishek Sethi, Sanchit Agarwal, Tagyoung Chung, and Dilek Hakkani-Tür. 2019. Dialog state tracking: A neural reading comprehension approach. In *Proceedings of the 20th Annual SIGdial Meeting on Discourse and Dialogue, SIGdial 2019, Stockholm, Sweden, September 11-13, 2019*, pages 264–273.

Rahul Goel, Shachi Paul, and Dilek Hakkani-Tür. 2019. Hyst: A hybrid approach for flexible and accurate dialogue state tracking. In *Interspeech 2019, 20th Annual Conference of the International Speech Communication Association, Graz, Austria, 15-19 September 2019*, pages 1458–1462.

Michael Heck, Carel van Niekerk, Nurul Lubis, Christian Geishauser, Hsien-Chin Lin, Marco Moresi, and Milica Gasic. 2020. Trippy: A triple copy strategy for value independent neural dialog state tracking. In *Proceedings of the 21th Annual Meeting of the Special Interest Group on Discourse and Dialogue, SIGdial 2020, 1st virtual meeting, July 1-3, 2020*, pages 35–44.

Yi Huang, Junlan Feng, Min Hu, Xiaoting Wu, Xiaoyu Du, and Shuo Ma. 2020. Meta-reinforced multi-domain state generator for dialogue systems. In *Proceedings of the 58th Annual Meeting of the Association for Computational Linguistics, ACL 2020, Online, July 5-10, 2020*, pages 7109–7118.

Mohit Iyyer, John Wieting, Kevin Gimpel, and Luke Zettlemoyer. 2018. Adversarial example generation with syntactically controlled paraphrase networks. In *Proceedings of the 2018 Conference of the North American Chapter of the Association for Computational Linguistics: Human Language Technologies, NAACL-HLT 2018, New Orleans, Louisiana, USA, June 1-6, 2018, Volume 1*, pages 1875–1885.

Di Jin, Zhijing Jin, Joey Tianyi Zhou, and Peter Szolovits. 2020. Is BERT really robust? A strong baseline for natural language attack on text classification and entailment. In *The Thirty-Fourth AAAI Conference on Artificial Intelligence, AAAI 2020, The Thirty-Second Innovative Applications of Artificial Intelligence Conference, IAAI 2020, The Tenth AAAI Symposium on Educational Advances in Artificial Intelligence, EAAI 2020, New York, NY, USA, February 7-12, 2020*, pages 8018–8025.

Hwaran Lee, Jinsik Lee, and Tae-Yoon Kim. 2019. SUMBT: slot-utterance matching for universal and scalable belief tracking. In *Proceedings of the 57th Conference of the Association for Computational Linguistics, ACL 2019, Florence, Italy, July 28- August 2, 2019, Volume 1: Long Papers*, pages 5478–5483.

Shiyang Li, Semih Yavuz, Kazuma Hashimoto, Jia Li, Tong Niu, Nazneen Fatema Rajani, Xifeng Yan, Yingbo Zhou, and Caiming Xiong. 2020. Coco: Controllable counterfactuals for evaluating dialogue state trackers. *CoRR*, abs/2010.12850.

Tal Linzen. 2020. How can we accelerate progress towards human-like linguistic generalization? In *Proceedings of the 58th Annual Meeting of the Association for Computational Linguistics, ACL 2020, Online, July 5-10, 2020*, pages 5210–5217.

Jun Quan and Deyi Xiong. 2020. Modeling long context for task-oriented dialogue state generation. In *Proceedings of the 58th Annual Meeting of the Association for Computational Linguistics, ACL 2020, Online, July 5-10, 2020*, pages 7119–7124. Association for Computational Linguistics.

Chien-Sheng Wu, Andrea Madotto, Ehsan Hosseini-Asl, Caiming Xiong, Richard Socher, and Pascale Fung. 2019. Transferable multi-domain state generator for task-oriented dialogue systems. In *Proceedings of the 57th Conference of the Association for Computational Linguistics, ACL 2019, Florence, Italy, July 28- August 2, 2019, Volume 1: Long Papers*, pages 808–819.

Dani Yogatama, Cyprien de Masson d'Autume, Jerome Connor, Tomás Kociský, Mike Chrzanowski, Lingpeng Kong, Angeliki Lazaridou, Wang Ling, Lei

Yu, Chris Dyer, and Phil Blunsom. 2019. Learning and evaluating general linguistic intelligence. *CoRR*, abs/1901.11373.

Jianguo Zhang, Kazuma Hashimoto, Chien-Sheng Wu, Yao Wan, Philip S. Yu, Richard Socher, and Caiming Xiong. 2019. Find or classify? dual strategy for slot-value predictions on multi-domain dialog state tracking. *CoRR*, abs/1910.03544.

GCDF1: A Goal- and Context- Driven F-Score for Evaluating User Models

Alexandru Coca, Bo-Hsiang Tseng, Bill Byrne
Department of Engineering, University of Cambridge, United Kingdom
`{ac2123, bht26, wjb31}@cam.ac.uk`

Abstract

The evaluation of dialogue systems in interaction with simulated users has been proposed to improve turn-level, corpus-based metrics which can only evaluate test cases encountered in a corpus and cannot measure system's ability to sustain multi-turn interactions. Recently, little emphasis was put on automatically assessing the quality of the user model itself, so unless correlations with human studies are measured, the reliability of user model based evaluation is unknown. We propose GCDF1, a simple but effective measure of the quality of semantic-level conversations between a goal-driven user agent and a system agent. In contrast with previous approaches we measure the F-score at dialogue level and consider user and system behaviours to improve recall and precision estimation. We facilitate scores interpretation by providing a rich hierarchical structure with information about conversational patterns present in the test data and tools to efficiently query the conversations generated. We apply our framework to assess the performance and weaknesses of a `Convlab2` user model[1].

1 Introduction

Remarkable progress has been achieved in many dialogue systems research disciplines, from dialogue state tracking (DST) (Dai et al., 2021; Mehri et al., 2020) to policy- (Wang et al., 2020; Lubis et al., 2020) and end-to-end modelling (Peng et al., 2021; Yang et al., 2020). Progress is usually measured *component-wise* through task-specific metrics and improvements in the overall performance of the systems leveraging advances in component designs are seldom reported (Takanobu et al., 2020). Takanobu et al. (2020) empirically show that component-wise evaluation may not correlate well with the overall performance of the system. They recommend evaluating dialogue systems in an end-to-end, interactive, *multi-turn* setting to capture the effect of error propagation on system performance and approximate the field performance of a system more accurately.

Takanobu et al. (2020) perform extensive user model interactive evaluation for a wide range of dialogue system architectures implemented in the `Convlab` library (Lee et al., 2019). They find that while the simulated user interaction evaluation overestimates the true performance of the systems evaluated, a mild correlation with human performance assessment exists. In this context, this paper seeks to provide a simple and effective tool to measure the predictive power of a user model, arguing that it is important to understand how well current user models perform and how to enhance them to improve system-wise evaluation accuracy.

We propose a simple generalisation of the corpus-based, turn-level F1 score proposed by Schatzmann et al. (2005) as a measure of the similarity between the (semantic-level) simulated user response and the response provided by a real user given the same context. We believe this to be necessary since turn-level F1 favours models which are biased to a potentially restricted set of behaviours learned from a corpus whereas an optimal user model should exhibit a wider variety of behaviours. Similar to the `Convlab2` (Zhu et al., 2020) evaluation, our metric is *goal-driven*. It evaluates, at *dialogue level*, the ability of the user model to express all the constraints[2] (I-GCDF1) and *request* all the information (R-GDCDF1) prescribed by a goal when interacting with an arbitrary agent. In human-human conversation, repetition of constraints occurs due to co-reference, confirmation, emphasis and through other linguistic and conversational processes. Information requests may be specified at the same time with the search constraints and later repeated. Language understanding errors may see agents stuck in conversational loops where

[1] Code available at `https://bit.ly/3hVS55Q`.

[2] A constraint (e.g., `price=cheap`) is formed of a *slot* which constrains the search (price) and its *value* (cheap).

Proceedings of the First Workshop on Evaluations and Assessments of Neural Conversation Systems, pages 7–14
Nov 11, 2021.

the same question and answer are repeated ad nauseam. Failure to account for these repetitions may thus affect F1 scores. Consequently, GCDF1 scores are also *context-driven*: the dialogue span between repetitions of constraints or requests is analysed to determine whether they are erroneous, elicited by a system behaviour, or due to an intrinsic user behaviour. In addition, the mentioning of *not-in-goal* constraints warranted by the conversational context (e.g., mentions of *don't care* values or entities) are accounted for.

The GCDF1 evaluator outputs a rich hierarchical structure where the interactions evaluated are classified according to the results of the context-driven analysis. Additionally, dialogue level score information and other metadata are output. We also developed tools to analyse evaluator output and query the set of interactions to interpret model behaviour. Hence, we hope that our implementation will help developers improve their models.

In summary, our contributions are:

- a dialogue-level, goal- and context-driven metric for evaluating the semantic interaction between a user- and a system model
- a reference implementation for the metric along with a set of tools that help developers interpret the results and find ways of improving their models.

We support these claims by studying the user model employed by Takanobu et al. (2020) in their study of dialogue system performance.

2 Related work

Schatzmann et al. (2005) propose a variety of turn- and dialogue-level statistics to compare generated and real corpora. The histograms of these statistics are used as proxies of user model performance. This is practical in the setting they analysed, but in general the high-dimensional nature of the data that may be extracted makes such comparisons difficult. Later work (Keizer et al., 2010; Cuayáhuitl et al., 2005) employed the Kullback-Leibler (KL) divergence to compare the distributions over extracted statistics. As well as posing estimation problems and being more sensitive to the means of the distributions compared to their shape, as a scalar measure, the KL divergence does not provide any insight into the structure of the generated data or how to improve the model. A divergence measure approach is also proposed by Williams (2007), who ranks user models according to the Cramér-von Mises divergence between the system performance distributions measured in interaction with simulated user populations and real users. Callejas et al. (2012) suggest to overcome the lack of interpretability of these apporaches by using mutidimensional subspace clustering to graphically show the similarity between generated and real data, but their metric is susceptible to the choice of features and clustering algorithm.

Jung et al. (2009) propose to adapt the BLEU score (Papineni et al., 2002) to capture "dialogue level naturalness" by considering a "gram" to be a user or system action and show that this metric correlates well with human judgement. One drawback to applying this metric to compare the sequences generated by user models with references is the arbitrary ordering of action sequences. The similarity of the simulated dialogues to the real data is assessed by evaluating the perplexity of the user model instead. However, this metric may not be a good indicator of the ability of the user model to predict a realistic response in an unknown dialogue situation, so it does not measure models' task completion ability.

To measure the ability to appropriately respond in a given dialogue situation, the turn-level F1 score (Schatzmann et al., 2005) is used. Alternatively, data is generated through interaction of the user model to be assessed with a wide range of system models, a protocol known as cross-evaluation (Schatztnann et al., 2005). System-side metrics of task success computed for each system model are then averaged and used as proxies for the user model performance: a good user model is expected to perform well when interacting with a variety of dialogue systems and should attain a high score.

3 Metric description

The following sections present the I- and R-GCDF1 algorithms. Our implementation is based on the MultiWOZ 2.1 (Eric et al., 2020) corpus, where the behaviours mentioned in this section were detected.

3.1 Inform-GCDF1 algorithm

To robustly measure the precision and recall of the user actions, the algorithm first maps the value in each constraint to its canonical form. It then accounts for not-in-goal constraints and system/user behaviours when counting constraint repetitions. Finally, it checks if missing user constraints have been preempted by the system.

Value normalisation MultiWOZ does not provide canonical value annotations. These are taken to be the values that parametrise the entire set of user goals. Value paraphrases of all the 17 informable slots are extracted from the dialogue acts, curated and mapped to canonical forms. This yields a mapping containing over $6,989$ surface form variations for $2,079$ canonical values. Even a simple slot such as area, which has only 5 canonical values was mapped to 239 distinct values. Not accounting for these surface forms variations would decrease I-GCDF1 accuracy because correct user constraints in non-canonical would be counted as false. It would also not be possible to accurately detect if the system pre-empts user constraints if the system constraints are not in canonical form positives.

The normalisation procedure uses the slot name to retrieve all the value paraphrases. The Levenshtein distance between a candidate value and each paraphrase is computed, and a paraphrase is considered a match its distance is less than 0.1. The canonical form of the value is the canonical form of the closest matching paraphrase within the aforementioned tolerance, if it exists.

Not-in-goal constraints A dialogue system might offer multiple entities that satisfy the informed constraints, so the user would have to provide the name to select one. The user may also provide the name when informed that their search did not return results and offered an alternative. The system may also specify entity attributes which are not in the goal that the user may co-refer to in the next turn. Finally, since it does not know the user goal, the system may request the user to provide values for slots outside it. These patterns are detected by the evaluator and the false positive counts are adjusted accordingly.

Constraints repetitions Constraint repetitions occur due to user and system behaviours. For example, if a user search or booking fails, the user may repeat some already mentioned information when updating their criteria. The system may also ask some values to be repeated if uncertain about what was communicated. In addition, the user might repeat information when stating new constraints, while discussing a potential transaction, when requesting information or responding to information requests. It is also possible that information is repeated when multiple domains are discussed simultaneously in one turn and the system only handles one domain in the following turn. Finally, repetitions due to system language understanding errors are also accounted for. If any of these behaviours occur, the evaluator allows up to `max_rep` repetitions before increasing false positive counts.

System constraint pre-emption The system is unaware of the user goal, so it may express some constraints before they can be provided by the user. The user may repeat some of them to confirm the values, but this may not necessarily occur since the user can accept a constraint through other mechanisms (e.g., acknowledgement, accepting an offer made at the same time). I-GCDF1 detects this system behaviour, adjusting the false negative counts.

3.2 R-GCDF1

Requests repetitions The user may repeat requests to overcome system language understanding errors. In addition to this, the algorithm also accounts for situations where the user informs the request before providing all the constraints and when the system omits responses. Up to `max_rep` per request are allowed before increasing the false positive counts when the repetition matches one of these patterns.

System request pre-emption Requests missing from user turns are searched in system turns to determine if the system has pre-empted the request by offering the information in advance (e.g., when confirming booking details or offering an entity).

4 Sample evaluation results

4.1 Experimental setup

System agent The system agent is a pipeline architecture implemented in the `Convlab2` library (Zhu et al., 2020). It is comprised of a BERT-based (Devlin et al., 2019) natural language understanding (NLU) module, a handcrafted policy, a rule-based DST and a retrieval natural language generation (NLG) module. This model outperforms all other `Convlab2` system configurations (Takanobu et al., 2020).

User agent We evaluate the architecture employed by Takanobu et al. (2020) in their user model based evaluation study. It is comprised of an MILU-based (Hakkani-Tür et al., 2016) NLU module, an agenda-based handcrafted policy (Schatzmann et al., 2007) and a retrieval NLG module.

Interaction setup We extend `Convlab2` by driving the interaction between the two agents by the MultiWOZ 2.1 test set goals (Figure 1). This facilitates comparisons with future work and is

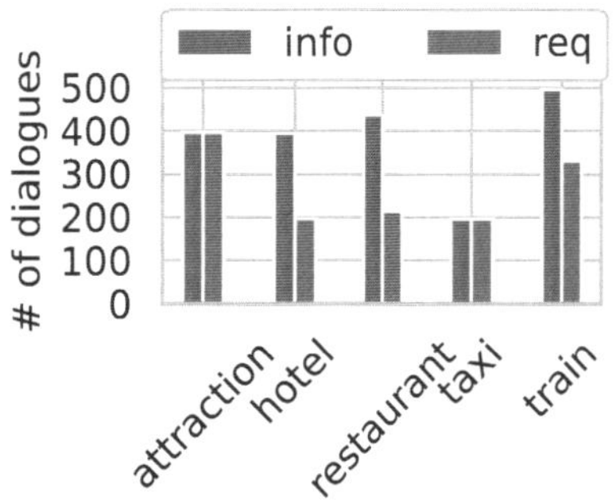

Figure 1: Domain distribution of the user goals in the MultiWOZ 2.1 test set

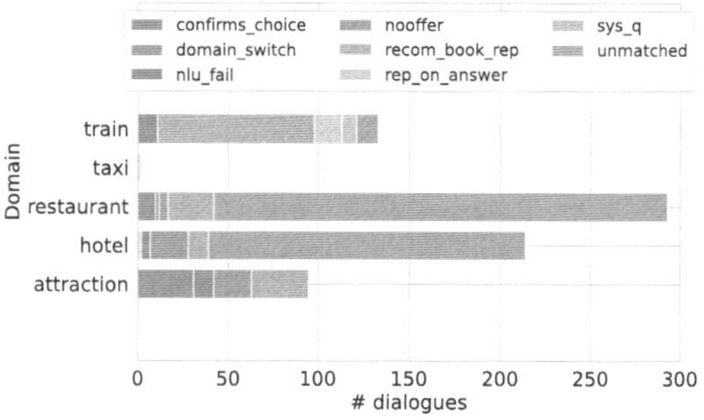

Figure 2: Prevalence of behaviours that lead to constraint repetitions

needed since the `Convlab2` goal model does not account for booking failures. The user and system agents interact freely until the conversation ends, for a maximum of 30 turns. The generated utterances, together with the user and system input and output actions are collected.

4.2 Behaviour and error states analysis

4.2.1 Constraints provision

The constraint provision ability of the user model varies significantly across the domains (Table 1).We explain these measurements in detail in the following section.

Domain	Combined	Attraction	Hotel	Restaurant	Taxi	Train
I-GCDF1	0.623	0.786	0.505	0.467	0.482	0.706

Table 1: I-GCDF1 scores. The combined score disregards domain information during counting.

Constraint repetitions Most commonly repetitions occur when the user discusses a booking or after a recommendation is made (Figure 2, `recom_book_rep`), a user behaviour which is detected by checking if the system has made a recommendation, offered an entity (i.e., presence of `{inform, select, recommend}(name|trainID=*)` actions) or prompted the user to make a booking (e.g., *Would you like to book a table?*). For the attraction domain, the slots `name, type` parametrise repeated constraints in 34 dialogues and in 3 diaologues repetitions are parametrised by the `area` slot. Analysis reveals that these repetitions are triggered by the MILU model, which generates the `request(name|type)` actions when encountering the phrases *Do you have any specific ideas in mind?* and *Anything in particular that you are looking for?*. Accordingly, the user say they don't care about the name or type of attraction. These questions are very frequently sampled by the NLG model, despite being superfluous: the user always provides enough constraints in the previous turns. The conversation only continues once the aforementioned sentences are not sampled. The NLU model also generates the `request(area)` action when the words *location, area* are mentioned in a response where the system intention is not to request information, so the user repeats the slot.

In the train domain, repetitions occur in 87 dialogues with the constraints on `day` slot being repeated in 86 of these, `departure` in 4 and `destination` only once. `day` is repeated so often because the systems' booking confirmation *Would you like to take the train on* `[day]?` is recognised as `request(day)` or `select(day=[day])`, which triggers the user policy to repeat the constraint. The NLU model does not correctly identify the `offerbooked`[3] dialogue act, which leads to this repetition pattern.

Repetition when answering a system request about a different slot (`rep_on_answer`) is not common and the system does not usually ask questions about constraints the user has already provided (`sys_q`). Additionaly, system understanding appears robust, and the user does not often have to re-provide information to overcome understanding errors. The user model repeats constraints when providing new information after the system informed the user they could not complete the current task with the specified constraints (`no_offer`).

A large number of repetitions are unmatched for the restaurant and hotel domains. For the former, in 251 dialogues (57.44% of di-

[3]This act annotates the booking details confirmation on the system side for the train domain.

alogues) these are *booking constraints* (i.e., which are parametrised by the slots `time, day, people`). The repetitions occur because the user model NLU mislabels the `restaurant-inform(reference=*)` action as `train-offerbooked(reference=*)`. This error causes the constraints to be repeated continuously until the dialogue session ends, so any domains that should have been discussed after the booking are missed, explaining the low taxi I-GCDF1 (Table 1). The issue occurs in the hotel domain for 96% of the 175 dialogues with constraint repetitions. The rest of the repetitions are of the `type=guesthouse` constraint, which the user repeats because the system responses to information requests contain the word *hotel* (e.g., *The hotel adress is* `[address]`*?*) which is interpreted as `inform(type=hotel)` by the NLU whereas the goal contains the `type=guesthouse` constraint.

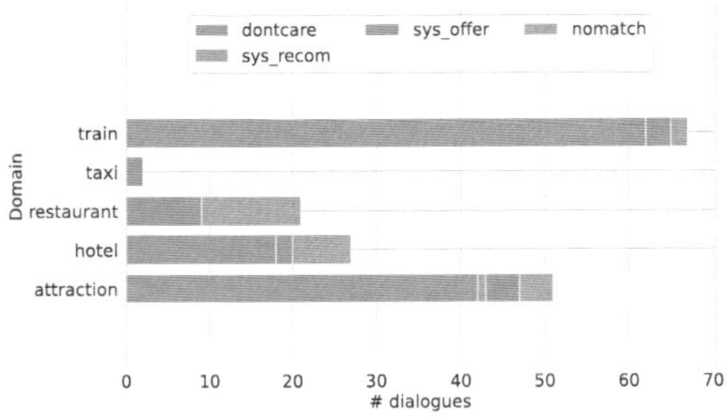

Figure 3: Not-in-goal constraints matching patterns

Not-in-goal constraints The user model frequently generates the `inform([slot_name]=dontcare)` action across all domains except restaurant (Figure 3). As discussed above, for the train and attraction domains these are triggered by the system language choice when confirming entity attributes. However, the slot-value `train-people=dontcare` is generated, suggesting that the model does not appropriately decline the system invitation to book train tickets. In the hotel domain, `dontcare` is generated to handle system requests of information not specified in the goal. In `sys_offer` conversations (Figure 3), the user model selects an entity by naming it or invites the system to choose an option for them by generating the action `inform(choice=any)`. In `notmatch` dialogues, the action `inform(notbook=none)` is generated by user model to decline reservation proposal. The evaluator does not match this act because the MultiWOZ 2.1 annotation system does not contain this slot-value pair. However, the evaluator has a configuration file where not-in-goal slot-value pairs that should be automatically matched can be listed, so modifying the algorithm to account for this situation, unknown at development time, is straightforward.

Constraint expression patterns Long sentences containing a lot of information are challenging for system NLU components. If all the information is provided at once, state tracking modules operating on NLU output are insufficiently tested. We analyse *constraints expression patterns* to understand whether all the search (or booking) constraints for a given domain are communicated in a single turn or across multiple turns.

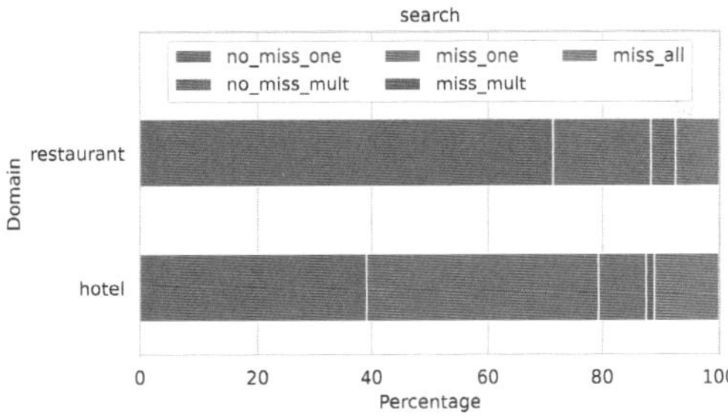

(a)

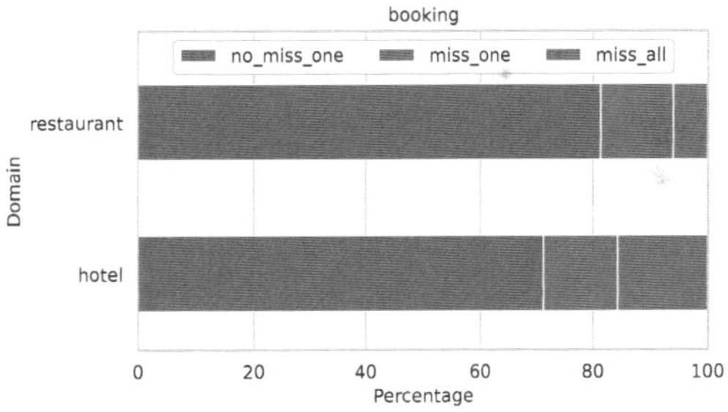

(b)

Figure 4: Constraint expression patterns. In `no*` dialogues all goal constraints have been communicated.

The user model is biased toward expressing all the search constraints at once (Figure 4a, `no_miss_one`) for the restaurant domain. Booking constraints are always expressed in the same turn. The baseline fails to search for an entity in just over 10% of the dialogues in the hotel domain and in close to 20% of the conversations in the same domain it does not attempt booking (Figure 4a, `miss_all`). In fact, Figure 5 shows that the baseline user model often fails to complete multi-

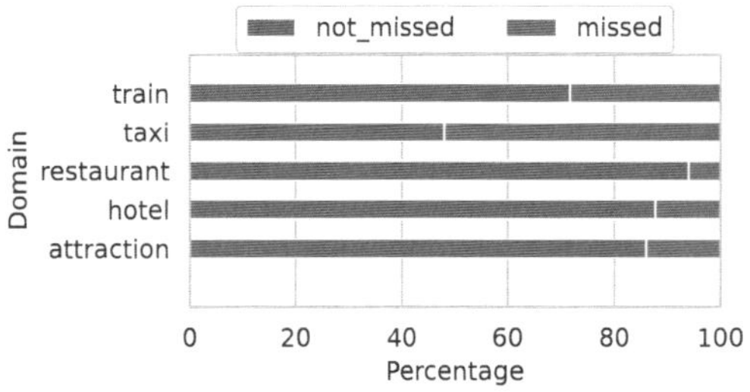

Figure 5: Percentage of dialogues where a domain in goal is not discussed by the baseline model

domain conversations. The taxi and train domains are frequently not discussed, explaining the poor performance reported in Table 1. Often, this is due to the failure of the NLU model to detect the `reference` and `entrance_fee` slots, which cause the user to indefinitely repeat the booking constraints or request the entrance fee. Hence, multi-domain dialogue simulation is very sensitive to natural language understanding capability.

Analysis of ability to request information

Model's ability to request information also varies significantly across domains (Table 2) and requests are always expressed in the same turn (Figure 6a).

Domain	Combined	Attraction	Hotel	Restaurant	Taxi	Train
R-GCDF1	0.692	0.719	0.770	0.873	0.482	0.658

Table 2: R-GCDF1 scores

The model either requests all information (`no_miss_one`), misses one or more requests (`miss_one`) or does not request any information (`miss_all_reqs`). The last pattern occurs because the two agents may get stuck in a question-answer loop. The `prov_all` category in Figure 6b shows the system may occasionally provides all the requests before the user can inform them. Taken together Figures 6a and 6b show that the user model makes all requests unless the system already provides the information: the scores in Table 2 are affected by the model's inability to complete multi-domain conversations and by requests repetition.

Figure 7 shows causes of requests repetition. The `delayed_resp` and `nlu_fail` categories contain the same dialogues, identifying conversations where the user model repeatedly requests information because the system does not immediately provide an answer. In `repeat_after_answer` dialogues user NLU errors for slots such as

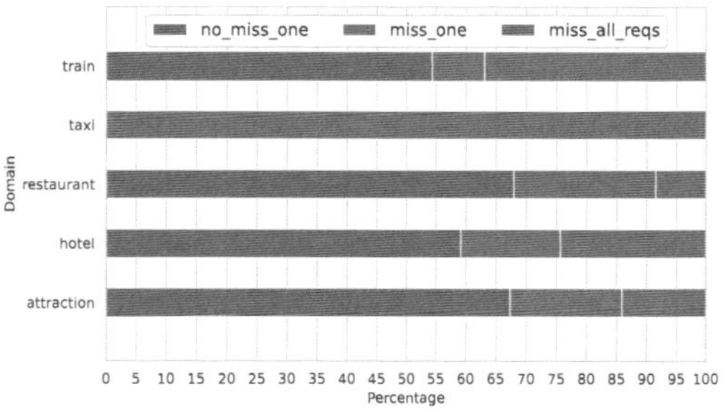

(a)

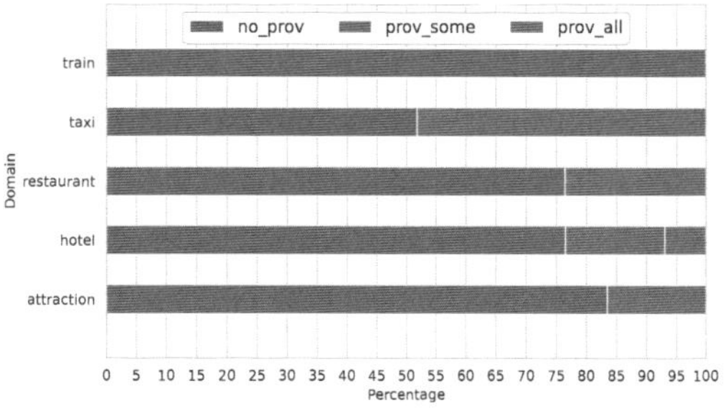

(b)

Figure 6: Requests expression patterns

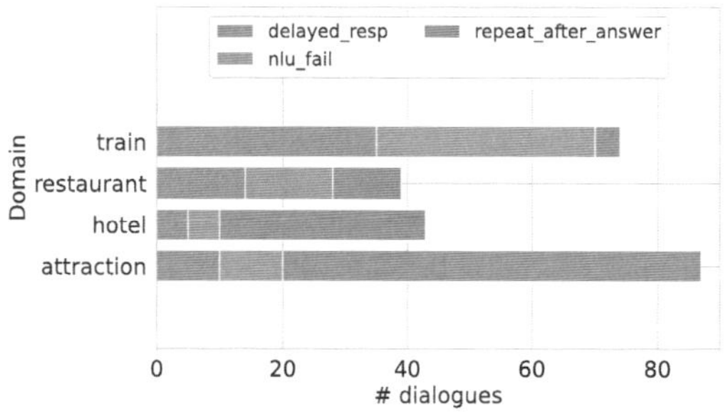

Figure 7: Information requests repetition reasons

`attraction-type` or `*-reference` lead to dialogue loops.

5 Conclusion

We proposed the GCDF1 framework and used it to conduct a detailed performance analysis of a user model. Understanding error states supports model improvement: for example, we identified that the user model analysed does not understand the `reference` slot. Hence, the user NLU model could be finetuned to resolve this error. The template NLG module was also shown to affect dialogue structure and quality. Future work could assess other `Convlab2` user models and extend our approach to larger corpora with more complex dialogue flows such as SGD (Rastogi et al., 2020).

Acknowledgements

This work was supported by EPSRC grant EP/R513180/1. Bo-Hsiang Tseng is supported by Cambridge Trust and the Ministry of Education, Taiwan.

References

Zoraida Callejas, David Griol, and Klaus-Peter Engelbrecht. 2012. Assessment of user simulators for spoken dialogue systems by means of subspace multidimensional clustering. In *INTERSPEECH 2012, 13th Annual Conference of the International Speech Communication Association, Portland, Oregon, USA, September 9-13, 2012*, pages 250–253. ISCA.

Heriberto Cuayáhuitl, Steve Renals, Oliver Lemon, and Hiroshi Shimodaira. 2005. Human-computer dialogue simulation using hidden markov models. In *IEEE Workshop on Automatic Speech Recognition and Understanding, 2005.*, pages 290–295. IEEE.

Yinpei Dai, Hangyu Li, Yongbin Li, Jian Sun, Fei Huang, Luo Si, and Xiaodan Zhu. 2021. Preview, attend and review: Schema-aware curriculum learning for multi-domain dialogue state tracking. In *Proceedings of the 59th Annual Meeting of the Association for Computational Linguistics and the 11th International Joint Conference on Natural Language Processing, ACL/IJCNLP 2021, (Volume 2: Short Papers), Virtual Event, August 1-6, 2021*, pages 879–885. Association for Computational Linguistics.

Jacob Devlin, Ming-Wei Chang, Kenton Lee, and Kristina Toutanova. 2019. BERT: pre-training of deep bidirectional transformers for language understanding. In *Proceedings of the 2019 Conference of the North American Chapter of the Association for Computational Linguistics: Human Language Technologies, NAACL-HLT 2019, Minneapolis, MN, USA, June 2-7, 2019, Volume 1 (Long and Short Papers)*, pages 4171–4186. Association for Computational Linguistics.

Mihail Eric, Rahul Goel, Shachi Paul, Abhishek Sethi, Sanchit Agarwal, Shuyang Gao, Adarsh Kumar ands Anuj Kumar Goyal, Peter Ku, and Dilek Hakkani-Tür. 2020. Multiwoz 2.1: A consolidated multi-domain dialogue dataset with state corrections and state tracking baselines. In *Proceedings of The 12th Language Resources and Evaluation Conference, LREC 2020, Marseille, France, May 11-16, 2020*, pages 422–428. European Language Resources Association.

Dilek Hakkani-Tür, Gökhan Tür, Asli Celikyilmaz, Yun-Nung Chen, Jianfeng Gao, Li Deng, and Ye-Yi Wang. 2016. Multi-domain joint semantic frame parsing using bi-directional RNN-LSTM. In *Interspeech 2016, 17th Annual Conference of the International Speech Communication Association, San Francisco, CA, USA, September 8-12, 2016*, pages 715–719. ISCA.

Sangkeun Jung, Cheongjae Lee, Kyungduk Kim, Minwoo Jeong, and Gary Geunbae Lee. 2009. Data-driven user simulation for automated evaluation of spoken dialog systems. *Computer Speech & Language*, 23(4):479–509.

Simon Keizer, Milica Gasic, Filip Jurcícek, François Mairesse, Blaise Thomson, Kai Yu, and Steve J. Young. 2010. Parameter estimation for agenda-based user simulation. In *Proceedings of the SIGDIAL 2010 Conference, The 11th Annual Meeting of the Special Interest Group on Discourse and Dialogue, 24-15 September 2010, Tokyo, Japan*, pages 116–123. The Association for Computer Linguistics.

Sungjin Lee, Qi Zhu, Ryuichi Takanobu, Zheng Zhang, Yaoqin Zhang, Xiang Li, Jinchao Li, Baolin Peng, Xiujun Li, Minlie Huang, and Jianfeng Gao. 2019. Convlab: Multi-domain end-to-end dialog system platform. In *Proceedings of the 57th Conference of the Association for Computational Linguistics, ACL 2019, Florence, Italy, July 28 - August 2, 2019, Volume 3: System Demonstrations*, pages 64–69. Association for Computational Linguistics.

Nurul Lubis, Christian Geishauser, Michael Heck, Hsien-Chin Lin, Marco Moresi, Carel van Niekerk, and Milica Gasic. 2020. LAVA: latent action spaces via variational auto-encoding for dialogue policy optimization. In *Proceedings of the 28th International Conference on Computational Linguistics, COLING 2020, Barcelona, Spain (Online), December 8-13, 2020*, pages 465–479. International Committee on Computational Linguistics.

Shikib Mehri, Mihail Eric, and Dilek Hakkani-Tür. 2020. Dialoglue: A natural language understanding benchmark for task-oriented dialogue. *CoRR*, abs/2009.13570.

Kishore Papineni, Salim Roukos, Todd Ward, and Wei-Jing Zhu. 2002. Bleu: a method for automatic evaluation of machine translation. In *Proceedings of the 40th Annual Meeting of the Association for Computational Linguistics, July 6-12, 2002, Philadelphia, PA, USA*, pages 311–318. ACL.

Baolin Peng, Chunyuan Li, Jinchao Li, Shahin Shayandeh, Lars Liden, and Jianfeng Gao. 2021. SOLOIST: building task bots at scale with transfer learning and machine teaching. *Trans. Assoc. Comput. Linguistics*, 9:907–824.

Abhinav Rastogi, Xiaoxue Zang, Srinivas Sunkara, Raghav Gupta, and Pranav Khaitan. 2020. Towards scalable multi-domain conversational agents: The schema-guided dialogue dataset. In *The Thirty-Fourth AAAI Conference on Artificial Intelligence, AAAI 2020, The Thirty-Second Innovative Applications of Artificial Intelligence Conference, IAAI 2020, The Tenth AAAI Symposium on Educational Advances in Artificial Intelligence, EAAI 2020, New*

York, NY, USA, February 7-12, 2020, pages 8689–8696. AAAI Press.

Jost Schatzmann, Kallirroi Georgila, and Steve J. Young. 2005. Quantitative evaluation of user simulation techniques for spoken dialogue systems. In *Proceedings of the 6th SIGdial Workshop on Discourse and Dialogue, SIGdial 2005, Lisbon, Portugal, 2-3 September 2005*, pages 45–54. Special Interest Group on Discourse and Dialogue (SIGdial).

Jost Schatzmann, Blaise Thomson, Karl Weilhammer, Hui Ye, and Steve J. Young. 2007. Agenda-based user simulation for bootstrapping a POMDP dialogue system. In *Human Language Technology Conference of the North American Chapter of the Association of Computational Linguistics, Proceedings, April 22-27, 2007, Rochester, New York, USA*, pages 149–152. The Association for Computational Linguistics.

Jost Schatztnann, Matthew N Stuttle, Karl Weilhammer, and Steve Young. 2005. Effects of the user model on simulation-based learning of dialogue strategies. In *IEEE Workshop on Automatic Speech Recognition and Understanding, 2005.*, pages 220–225. IEEE.

Ryuichi Takanobu, Qi Zhu, Jinchao Li, Baolin Peng, Jianfeng Gao, and Minlie Huang. 2020. Is your goal-oriented dialog model performing really well? empirical analysis of system-wise evaluation. In *Proceedings of the 21th Annual Meeting of the Special Interest Group on Discourse and Dialogue, SIGdial 2020, 1st virtual meeting, July 1-3, 2020*, pages 297–310. Association for Computational Linguistics.

Kai Wang, Junfeng Tian, Rui Wang, Xiaojun Quan, and Jianxing Yu. 2020. Multi-domain dialogue acts and response co-generation. In *Proceedings of the 58th Annual Meeting of the Association for Computational Linguistics, ACL 2020, Online, July 5-10, 2020*, pages 7125–7134. Association for Computational Linguistics.

Jason D. Williams. 2007. A method for evaluating and comparing user simulations: The cramér-von mises divergence. In *IEEE Workshop on Automatic Speech Recognition & Understanding, ASRU 2007, Kyoto, Japan, December 9-13, 2007*, pages 508–513. IEEE.

Yunyi Yang, Yunhao Li, and Xiaojun Quan. 2020. UBAR: towards fully end-to-end task-oriented dialog systems with GPT-2. *CoRR*, abs/2012.03539.

Qi Zhu, Zheng Zhang, Yan Fang, Xiang Li, Ryuichi Takanobu, Jinchao Li, Baolin Peng, Jianfeng Gao, Xiaoyan Zhu, and Minlie Huang. 2020. Convlab-2: An open-source toolkit for building, evaluating, and diagnosing dialogue systems. In *Proceedings of the 58th Annual Meeting of the Association for Computational Linguistics: System Demonstrations, ACL 2020, Online, July 5-10, 2020*, pages 142–149. Association for Computational Linguistics.

A Comprehensive Assessment of Dialog Evaluation Metrics

Yi-Ting Yeh, Maxine Eskenazi, Shikib Mehri
Language Technologies Institute, Carnegie Mellon University
{yitingye,max,amehri}@cs.cmu.edu

Abstract

Automatic evaluation metrics are a crucial component of dialog systems research. Standard language evaluation metrics are known to be ineffective for evaluating dialog. As such, recent research has proposed a number of novel, dialog-specific metrics that correlate better with human judgements. Due to the fast pace of research, many of these metrics have been assessed on different datasets and there has as yet been no time for a systematic comparison between them. To this end, this paper provides a comprehensive assessment of recently proposed dialog evaluation metrics on a number of datasets. In this paper, 23 different automatic evaluation metrics are evaluated on 10 different datasets. Furthermore, the metrics are assessed in different settings, to better qualify their respective strengths and weaknesses. This comprehensive assessment offers several takeaways pertaining to dialog evaluation metrics in general. It also suggests how to best assess evaluation metrics and indicates promising directions for future work.

1 Introduction

Evaluation is a crucial component of the research process. Evaluation metrics are used to shine light on the best models and thus they strongly influence the research directions of a field. Standard automatic language evaluation metrics (e.g., BLEU, METEOR) have been shown to be ineffective for evaluating dialog (Liu et al., 2016b; Deriu et al., 2021). To this end, recent research has proposed a number of automatic metrics specifically designed to evaluate dialog (Tao et al., 2018; Ghazarian et al., 2019; Lan et al., 2020; Pang et al., 2020; Ghazarian et al., 2020; Sinha et al., 2020; Huang et al., 2020; Mehri and Eskenazi, 2020b,a; Zhang et al., 2021b). These metrics address the weaknesses of the standard language evaluation metrics. They have also been shown to better correlate with human judgement. However, most of these metrics were developed at about the same time and were evaluated on different datasets. As such, there has not yet been a consistent comparison amongst them. This paper describes an assessment of these metrics on several different datasets. It quantifies the relative performance and reveals strengths and weaknesses of each metric.

Due to the fact that standard automatic metrics have been shown to be ineffective for dialog evaluation (Liu et al., 2016b; Deriu et al., 2021), dialog research typically relies on human evaluation. While useful and very informative, human evaluation is expensive and time-consuming. Given these considerations, at present it is usually only used for a final evaluation. Yet, during the development process, automatic evaluation metrics are essential since they are used to optimize the model design and the choice of hyperparameters. In order to be relevant and meaningful, these metrics must better correlate with human judgment so that they serve as a meaningful proxy for human judgements during the development process.

This paper discusses the assessment of several recently-proposed automatic evaluation metrics for dialog over several datasets. These datasets have human annotations that measure the quality of the responses. Furthermore, this paper includes analysis experiments that qualify the performance of the metrics across different settings. This assessment measures the performance of the metrics (1) on both the turn level and the dialog level, (2) for different dialog lengths, (3) for different dialog qualities (e.g., coherence, engaging), (4) for different types of response generation models (i.e., generative, retrieval, simple models and state-of-the-art models), and (5) exploring combinations of different metrics.

All of the code created for this assessment is open-sourced[1] to facilitate the easy assessment of

[1] https://github.com/exe1023/DialEvalMetrics

Proceedings of the First Workshop on Evaluations and Assessments of Neural Conversation Systems, pages 15–33

future evaluation metrics on a number of datasets.

2 Overview of Automatic Metrics

In this paper, we studied 23 automatic metrics either designed for evaluating dialogues or general natural language generation (NLG) tasks. Table 1 presents an overview of metrics. Besides model designs and training objectives, the three aspects used to characterize them are: (1) Does the metric use a pretrained language model? (2) What data was used to train the metric? (3) Does the metric require a reference response or is it reference-free?

In most metrics, triplet ranking loss is used as a training objective, and it requires the model to give higher scores to appropriate responses. BERT (Devlin et al., 2019) and its variant RoBERTa (Liu et al., 2019) are the most popular pretrained language models utilized in state-of-the-art metrics, followed by GPT-2 language model (Radford et al., 2019). DailyDialog (Li et al., 2017) and PersonaChat (Zhang et al., 2018) are two widely-used datasets for training metrics. Briefly, conversation topics of DailyDialog are about day-to-day life, while Personachat consists of dialogs where each participant is assigned a persona and the goal is to become familiar with the other individual. Word-overlap metrics are ineffective for dialog (Liu et al., 2016b) largely due to the one-to-many nature of dialog (Zhao et al., 2017a). Thus, reference-free metrics have been proposed to circumvent the one-to-many problem. Amongst the 24 metrics assessed here, we have 11 reference-free evaluation metrics.

We refer readers to Appendix A for detailed discussion of aforementioned characteristics of assessed metrics.

3 Testing Datasets

In this work, we test metrics with the quality annotated datasets: USR (Mehri and Eskenazi, 2020b), GRADE (Huang et al., 2020), HolisticEval (Pang et al., 2020), FED (Mehri and Eskenazi, 2020a), DSTC6 (Hori and Hori, 2017) and DSTC9 (Gunasekara et al., 2021). Concretely, each sample in the dataset consists of a dialog context, a generated response and a quality score. Optionally, a ground-truth response may also be included. Due to the space constraint, in this section we only provide a high-level overview of the used datasets. The complete list and discussion of characteristics of used datasets is provided in Appendix B.

In general, these datasets are constructed using the following steps:

1. Choose an existing dialog dataset.
2. Train a response generation model on the chosen dialog dataset.
3. Generate responses for the validation/test set of the chosen dataset
4. Collect human quality annotations for the generated responses.

For data that does not contain referenced responses, only reference-free metrics were assessed.

The characteristics of the quality-annotated data significantly influence the performance of the metrics since dialog metrics might be originally developed and trained on data in a very different domain than the test domain. For example, since many of these datasets were collected in different settings, they have diverse formality, complexity of the sentence structure, and the dialog length. Despite using the same underlying dialog dataset, the response generation model used would also influence the characteristics of responses. Distinguishing between responses with very different quality is easier, since the low quality response may not even follow grammar rules or the dialog context. On the other hand, it will be challenging to give appropriate scores to responses from state-of-the-art dialog systems. In the 10 datasets, responses in the data labeled by GRADE, FED, and DSTC9 data come from models with relatively better empirical performance such as Transformer Seq2Seq model (Vaswani et al., 2017), DialoGPT (Zhang et al., 2020), and Meena (Adiwardana et al., 2020b).

4 Experiments

This section describes the assessment of the evaluation metrics. Wherever possible, the released pretrained model was used to reproduce results. Since RUBER, BERT-RUBER and PONE do not release their pretrained models, those models were trained on DailyDialog. For USR, we use the released model which is trained on TopicalChat. For PredictiveEngage, the original paper combined the model with RUBER for the best performance. In this assessment only the engagement score model is used for comparison to the other metrics. FlowScore only scores dialogs with more than 3 utterances, so it cannot be used on some of the quality-annotated data.

Metric	Pretrained Model	Training Dataset	Reference-Free?	Objective
BLEU (2002)	X	X	X	X
METEOR (2005)	X	X	X	X
ROUGE (2004)	X	X	X	X
ADEM (2017)	X	Ubuntu Dialogue + Twitter	X	MSE
BERTScore (2019)	BERT	X	X	X
BLEURT (2020)	BERT	WMT Metrics Shared Task	X	MSE
QuestEval (2021)	T5	SQuAD-v2/NewsQA	√	QA/QG
RUBER (2018)	X	DailyDialog / PersonaChat	X	Triplet
BERT-RUBER (2019)	BERT	DailyDialog / PersonaChat	X	Triplet
PONE (2020)	BERT	DailyDialog	X	Triplet
MAUDE (2020)	BERT	PersonaChat	√	NCE
DEB (2020)	BERT	Reddit/DailyDialog++	√	MLM/NSP
GRADE (2020)	BERT	DailyDialog	√	Triplet
DynaEval (2021a)	RoBERTa	ED/ConvAI2/DailyDialog	√	Triplet
USR (2020b)	RoBERTa	TopicalChat / PersonaChat	√	MLM/CrossEntropy
USL-H (2020)	BERT	DailyDialog	√	VUP/NSP/MLM
DialogRPT (2020)	GPT-2	Reddit	√	CrossEntropy
Deep AM-FM (2021b)	Multilingual BERT	Twitter	X	MLM
HolisticEval (2020)	BERT	DailyDialog	√	LM
PredictiveEngage (2020)	BERT	ConvAI	X	CrossEntropy
FED (2020a)	DialoGPT	X	√	X
FlowScore (2021b)	Plato	Reddit	√	ContextFlow
FBD (2021)	RoBERTa	X	X	X

Table 1: Summary of the evaluation metrics assessed in this paper. The 'Pretrained Model' column indicates the specific pretrained language model used by the metric. The 'Training Dataset' and 'Objective' columns describe the dialog data and the objective used when training the metric. 'Reference-Free?' indicates whether the metric requires a reference response for evaluation. ED is the abbreviation of the EmpatheticDialogue dataset.

4.1 Results on Datasets with Human Reference

This section describes the performance of the metrics on the quality-annotated datasets that contain a human reference. This distinction is important, because the referenced metrics (e.g., BLEU, METEOR, BERTScore) can only be assessed on these datasets. Table 2 present the correlations of the metrics on the USR, GRADE, and DSTC6 data. Due to the space constraint, we only present Spearman correlation, and the full table could be found in Appendix C.

Rule-based metrics perform surprisingly well on USR-TopicalChat and USR-PersonaChat. However, they fall short on the GRADE data. This may be due to the fact that the responses in the GRADE data are produced by better NLG models, as described in Section 3. Since rule-based metrics calculate word-overlap metrics between the system responses and a human reference, they can consistently detect poor responses which only contain irrelevant words. However, the rule-based metrics struggle to score responses from state-of-the-art dialog systems since those responses require a deeper semantic understanding of the dialog context and the generated response.

USR, GRADE, DEB, and USL-H are the best performing metrics for evaluating response generation (i.e., turn-level correlation). The USR and GRADE metrics have high performance on their respective datasets. This phenomenon probably occurs for several reasons. First, both metrics finetune pretrained models in a self-supervised manner on certain dialog datasets. It is expected that the metrics would perform better on quality-annotated datasets corresponding to the data they were finetuned on. For example, the choice of the topic graph of GRADE may have been influenced by phenomena observed in the GRADE data. Finally, metrics may be optimized specifically for the data (i.e., through hyperparameter tuning on a validation set). This observation stresses the importance of testing on a variety of different quality-annotated datasets in order to ensure the generality of an evaluation metric and to avoid over-optimizing to specific datasets.

The performance of DEB demonstrates the importance of training data in model-based metrics. DEB replaces the BERT pretraining data with a dialog corpus, and further finetunes the model on a manually-created dataset consisting of adversarial responses designed for the NSP objective. USL-H has a similar performance trend to USR, which is reasonable since the two metrics both combine response selection models and language models. The VUP model which validates whether a given response is grammatically correct helps USL-H outperforms USR on the USR-PersonaChat dataset.

4.2 Results on Datasets without Human Reference

This section describes the results for the datasets that do not contain a reference response. Only reference-free metrics can be evaluated on these quality-annotated datasets.

Table 3 presents results of the reference-free

	USR-TopicalChat		USR-PersonaChat		GRADE-ConvAI2		GRADE-DD		GRADE-ED		DSTC6	
	Turn	System	Turn	System	Turn	System	Turn	System	Turn	System	Turn	System
BLEU-4	0.296	0.900	0.090*	0.800*	0.128	0.000*	0.184	**1.000**	0.002*	**1.000**	0.298	0.050*
METEOR	0.391	0.900	0.271	0.800*	0.181	0.600*	0.010*	-1.000	0.055*	**1.000**	0.323	0.084*
ROUGE-L	0.287	0.900	0.038*	0.000*	0.140	0.000*	0.147	**1.000**	-0.013*	**1.000**	0.326	0.215*
ADEM	-0.061*	0.700*	-0.085*	0.400*	-0.057*	-0.200*	0.071*	**1.000**	-0.028*	**1.000**	0.118	0.347*
BERTScore	0.325	0.900	0.122*	0.000*	0.224	0.800*	0.100*	-1.000	0.033*	**1.000**	**0.337**	0.265*
BLEURT	0.261	0.900	0.054*	0.000*	0.120	-0.400*	0.133	**1.000**	0.051*	**1.000**	0.294	0.426*
QuestEval	0.338	**1.000**	0.236	**1.000**	0.319	0.400*	0.006*	-1.000	0.272	**1.000**	0.242	0.206*
RUBER	0.259	**1.000**	0.190	**1.000**	-0.042*	-0.400*	-0.094*	-1.000	-0.039*	**1.000**	0.092	0.104*
BERT-RUBER	0.348	0.900	0.248	0.200*	0.314	**1.000**	0.128	-1.000	0.148	**1.000**	0.217	0.093*
PONE	0.274	0.500*	0.375	0.800*	0.373	0.800*	0.163	-1.000	0.161	**1.000**	0.200	0.235*
MAUDE	0.083*	-0.200*	0.298	0.400*	0.304	0.800*	-0.073*	**1.000**	-0.057*	**1.000**	0.128	0.217*
DEB	0.116	0.400*	0.373	**1.000**	0.504	**1.000**	**0.363**	1.000	**0.395**	**1.000**	0.214	0.492
GRADE	0.217	0.100*	0.352	**1.000**	**0.571**	0.800*	0.253	-1.000	0.297	**1.000**	0.122	0.611
DynaEval	-0.022*	0.100*	0.171	0.800*	0.131	-1.000	0.120	-1.000	0.141	-1.000	0.246	-0.050*
USR	**0.423**	0.900	0.418	**1.000**	0.500	**1.000**	0.057*	-1.000	0.255	**1.000**	0.166	0.147*
USL-H	0.340	0.900	**0.523**	0.800*	0.457	1.000	0.093*	-1.000	0.235	**1.000**	0.179	0.298*
DialogRPT	0.105*	0.600*	-0.083*	0.800*	0.158	-0.600*	0.037*	-1.000	0.203	1.000	0.155	0.334*
Deep AM-FM	0.268	0.700*	0.219	**1.000**	0.130	0.400*	0.022*	**1.000**	0.058*	**1.000**	0.295	**0.674**
HolisticEval	-0.123	-0.200*	0.113*	0.000*	-0.010*	-0.400*	0.020*	**1.000**	0.204	-1.000	-0.004*	-0.002
PredictiveEngage	0.310	0.900	0.033*	0.200*	0.164	0.600*	-0.135	-1.000	-0.078*	**1.000**	0.004*	-0.409*
FED	-0.135	0.100*	-0.000*	0.400*	-0.072*	0.000*	0.064*	**1.000**	-0.044*	**1.000**	-0.083	0.322*
FlowScore	0.082*	0.400*	0.079*	0.800*	-	-	-	-	-	-	0.095	0.362*
FBD	-	0.100*	-	0.800*	-	-0.400*	-	-1.000	-	-1.000	-	-0.234*
GRADE + DEB	0.217	0.400*	0.403	1.000	0.549	1.000	0.325	1.000	0.391	1.000	0.200	0.501
USR + USL + GRADE + DEB	0.382	0.700*	0.495	1.000	0.579	1.000	0.198	-1.000	0.387	1.000	0.238	0.553
ALL	0.473	0.900	0.534	1.000	0.561	1.000	0.149	-1.000	0.349	1.000	0.268	0.761

Table 2: Results on datasets with human reference. All values are statistically significant to $p < 0.05$, unless marked by *. GRADE-DD and GRADE-ED indicate the GRADE-DailyDialog and GRADE-EmpatheticDialogue dataset, respectively. PE is the abbreviation of PredictiveEngage metric.

	PE-DailyDialog		FED				DSTC9			
	Turn-Level		Turn-Level		Dialog-Level		Dialog-Level		System-Level	
	P	S	P	S	P	S	P	S	P	S
QuestEval	0.296	0.341	0.037*	0.093*	-0.032*	0.080*	0.026*	0.043	0.604	0.527*
MAUDE	0.104	0.060*	0.018*	-0.094*	-0.047*	-0.280	0.059	0.042*	0.224*	0.045*
DEB	0.516	0.580	0.230	0.187	-0.130*	0.006*	0.085	0.131	0.683	0.473*
GRADE	0.600	0.622	0.134	0.118	-0.034*	-0.065*	-0.078	-0.070	-0.674	-0.482*
DynaEval	0.167	0.160	**0.319**	**0.323**	**0.503**	**0.547**	0.093	0.101	0.652	0.727
USR	0.582	0.640	0.114	0.117	0.093*	0.062*	0.019*	0.020*	0.149*	0.127*
USL-H	**0.688**	**0.699**	0.201	0.189	0.073*	0.152*	0.105	0.105	0.566*	0.755
DialogRPT	0.489	0.533	-0.118	-0.086*	-0.221	-0.214	0.076	0.069	0.685	0.555*
HolisticEval	0.368	0.365	0.122	0.125	-0.276	-0.304	0.015*	0.002*	-0.019*	-0.100*
PredictiveEngage	0.429	0.414	0.024*	0.094*	0.026*	0.155*	0.114	0.115	0.809	0.664
FED	0.164	0.159	0.120	0.095	0.222	0.320	0.128	0.120	0.559*	0.391*
FlowScore	-	-	-0.065*	-0.055*	-0.073*	-0.003*	**0.147**	**0.140**	**0.907**	**0.900**
FBD	-	-	-	-	-	-	-	-	-0.669	-0.627

Table 3: Results on PredictiveEngage-DailyDialog, FED, and DSTC9 data. P and S indicate Pearson correlation and Spearman correlation, respectively. Here, we denote PredictiveEngage-DailyDialog by PE-DailyDialog due to space constraint. All values are statistically significant to $p < 0.05$, unless marked by *.

metrics on HolisticEval-DailyDialog, FED, and DSTC9 data.

In the FED dataset, there are two types of annotations: turn-level and dialog-level. Turn-level annotations assess the quality of a single response, while dialog-level annotations assess the entire dialog. Similar to the GRADE data, the responses in the FED data are generated by state-of-the-art dialog systems (Adiwardana et al., 2020b), which makes the data particularly challenging.

Many metrics which perform well on the USR and GRADE data, do not do as well on the FED data. This may be because of the longer dialog context in the FED data. While the average number of words in the context of GRADE-ConvAI2 is 23.4, the context of FED has on average 86.5 words and 11.8 utterances. If a model has not seen long contexts at training time, it will struggle to perform well on longer contexts at test time.

FlowScore, PredictiveEngage, DynaEval and FED perform the best on dialog-level evaluation on the FED and DSTC9 datasets. This may occur for two reasons. First, these models are designed to capture properties that are better aligned with dialog-level annotations: FlowScore models the dynamic infor- mation flow in the dialog history, DynaEval measures coherence using a graph-based representation of the dialog, PredictiveEngage measures engagement, FED measures a number of different dialog-level qualities (e.g., coherence, topic depth, etc.). Second, the model architectures of PredictiveEngage and FED are relatively simple. This may make the two metrics less sensitive to longer dialog contexts. Though these metrics do well at assessing state-of-the-art dialog systems in the FED and DSTC9 data, they underperform on the GRADE and USR data. This suggests that these two metrics are optimal for dialog-level evaluation, but less so for turn-level evaluation.

4.3 Results on System-Level Correlation

This section presents system-level correlation on quality-annotated datasets. System-level correlation is a strong indication of the ability of metrics to rank several response generation models. GRADE-DailyDialog and GRADE-EmpatheticDialog only consist of 2 systems, which makes system-level correlation much less informative.

In general, metrics that have a higher turn-level correlation tend to have a higher system-level correlation. Interestingly, some metrics which perform poorly on turn-level correlation do much better on system-level correlation, suggesting that averaging out over all the examples produced by a dialog system reduces the noise in the metric's scores. For example, GRADE has a comparable system-level correlation to the best-performing Deep AM-FM on the DSTC6 data, despite having a lower turn-level correlation. On the other hand, BERTScore, which has the highest turn-level correlation on the DSTC6 data, performs poorly on system-level correlation. This suggests that word-overlap metrics may struggle to accurately assess entire systems.

System-level correlations are generally very strong across a variety of metrics. Most impressively are the high correlations of Deep AM-FM on the DSTC6 data (11 different systems) and of FlowScore on the DSTC9 data (20 different systems).

4.4 Performance on Various Dialog Qualities

Since dialog quality is inherently multi-faceted (Walker et al., 1997; See et al., 2019), it is inadequate to only evaluate dialog metrics on the overall response score. Therefore, this paper also presents the correlation of the metrics with various dialog qualities in Table 4 and Figure 1.

HolisticEval-DailyDialog annotates the context coherence of responses. For the FED data, we present results on 8 fine-grained turn-level qualitites, and results on dialog-level qualities could be found in Appendix. For metrics that produce fine-grained scores, we use the corresponding fine-grained score to measure correlation. For example, because PredictiveEngage evaluates the engaging quality of the dialog, the *engaging* score, rather than the overall score, is used to measure correlation with the *engaging* quality in the FED dataset.

USR and USL-H both do well predicting context coherence and engaging on the HolisticEval-DailyDialog and FED data, respectively. These two metrics also have good performance on the USR and GRADE data. In contrast, HolisticEval and PredictiveEngage do well on measuring coherence and engagement, but underperform on the USR and GRADE data. This suggests that while fine-grained metrics are important qualities to measure, modelling *only* these qualities is insufficient. Instead, it is better to design a metric that measures many different qualities and can aggregate them to form an overall score, such as the combination of MLM/dialog retrieval in USR and MLM/VUP/NSP in USL-H. *The evaluation of specific fine-grained qualities sheds much light on their underlying behavior.*

	HolisticEval-DailyDialog	
	Pearson	Spearman
QuestEval	0.285	0.260
MAUDE	0.275	0.364
DEB	0.584	0.663
GRADE	**0.678**	0.697
DynaEval	-0.023*	-0.009*
USR	0.589	0.645
USL-H	0.486	0.537
DialogRPT	0.283	0.332
HolisticEval	0.670	**0.764**
PredictiveEngage	-0.033*	0.060*
FED	0.485	0.507
FlowScore	-	-
FBD	-	-

Table 4: Results on HolisticEval-DailyDialog. All values are statistically significant to $p < 0.05$, unless marked by *.

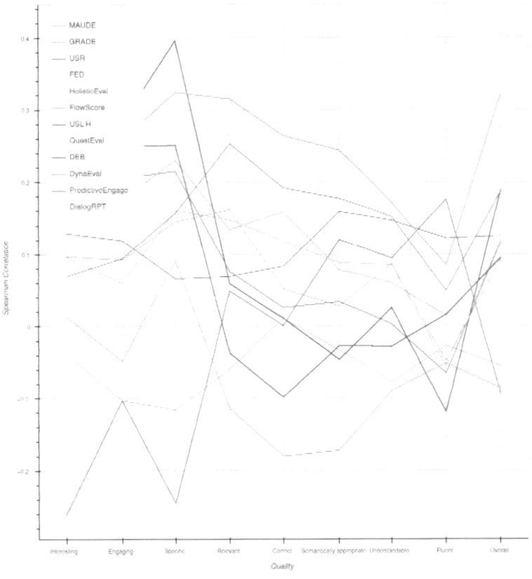

Figure 1: Spearman correlation to different turn-level annotation qualities on the FED data.

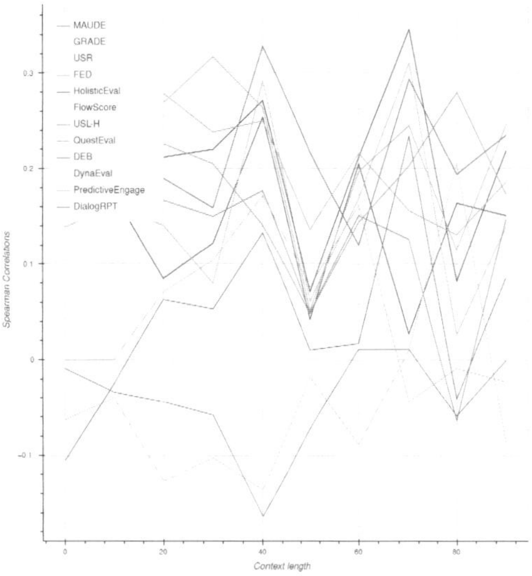

Figure 2: Spearman correlation when varying the dialog context length.

4.5 Effect of Context Length

Most reference-free metrics compute their scores by comparing the dialog context with the response. Therefore, it is interesting to determine if these metrics perform differently according to the length of the dialog context. The quality-annotated samples are grouped by their context lengths with a length interval of 10. Figure 2 shows performance differences of the reference-free metrics at different context lengths.

Many metrics' performance decreases as the context lengthens. This may be due to the fact that those metrics are trained on shorter dialogs and struggle to understand longer dialog contexts. On the other hand, the performance of HolisticEval, DialogRPT, and FED increases as the context lengthens. These metrics incorporate GPT-2-based language models to score responses, while the other metrics mostly rely on BERT-based models. BERT-based models are optimized for local coherence on the BookCorpus and Wikipedia through the MLM objective and limit context length. Thus GPT-2-based metrics perform better on longer dialogs.

The performance of USL-H, DEB, and PredictiveEngage does not change much at different context lengths. For PredictiveEngage, this could be because PredictiveEngage uses several MLP layers during the pooling of the pretrained BERT embeddings to predict the output. USL-H uses the VUP model which aims to determine if a response is grammatically correct. The use of the VUP model may make USL-H robust to longer context lengths. The BERT model used in DEB is pretrained on the Reddit corpus which may improve its ability to model long-range correlations in the dialog. These different factors make metrics more robust to different context lengths.

4.6 Combining Metrics

Many metrics rely on an ensemble of different models. Inspired by this, this section explores the possibility that a combination of metrics may be successful (Table 2). Since it is not feasible to exhaustively explore all possible combinations of the metrics, some combinations of the best-performing metrics were explored here. The metrics are combined through simple averaging. *Future work should explore more sophisticated mechanisms for combining metrics.*

In the last three rows of Table 2, we selectively present the three combinations of metrics with the best performance. The complete table and discussion could be found in Appendix C.3. In general, combinations of the best performing metrics USR, GRADE, USL-H, and DEB improve the performance. The last row shows results of taking the average of the scores of all of the metrics that were assessed in this paper. While the idea of an *All* metric is simple, and metrics are combined through simple averaging, the results are surprisingly good across the different referenced quality-annotated datasets. This result highlights the potential of combining various evaluation metrics in better manners.

5 Conclusions

This paper provides a comprehensive assessment of various automatic evaluation metrics for dialog. Many different evaluation metrics have been proposed in recent years. The results indicate several important directions for future work on the assessment of dialog evaluation metrics: 1) Many metrics rely on pretrained language models, and the analysis in this paper highlights the impacts of them. Researchers could further explore the impact of choice of pretrianed models. 2) Unsurprisingly, Metrics generally perform better on the data they were trained on. Therefore, methods to adapt metrics to new domains should be an important research direction. 3) Simple combinations of metrics yield promising results. Future work should explore more sophisticated ways for combining metrics.

6 Acknowledgements

We thank the authors of the various metrics for releasing their code. This work is funded by National Science Foundation grant CNS-1512973. The opinions expressed in this paper do not necessarily reflect those of the National Science Foundation.

References

D. Adiwardana, Minh-Thang Luong, David R. So, J. Hall, Noah Fiedel, R. Thoppilan, Z. Yang, Apoorv Kulshreshtha, Gaurav Nemade, Yifeng Lu, and Quoc V. Le. 2020a. Towards a human-like open-domain chatbot. *ArXiv*, abs/2001.09977.

Daniel Adiwardana, Minh-Thang Luong, David R So, Jamie Hall, Noah Fiedel, Romal Thoppilan, Zi Yang, Apoorv Kulshreshtha, Gaurav Nemade, Yifeng Lu, et al. 2020b. Towards a human-like open-domain chatbot. *arXiv preprint arXiv:2001.09977*.

R Ananthakrishnan, Pushpak Bhattacharyya, M Sasikumar, and Ritesh M Shah. 2007. Some issues in automatic evaluation of english-hindi mt: more blues for bleu. *ICON*.

Satanjeev Banerjee and Alon Lavie. 2005. METEOR: An automatic metric for MT evaluation with improved correlation with human judgments. In *Proceedings of the ACL Workshop on Intrinsic and Extrinsic Evaluation Measures for Machine Translation and/or Summarization*, pages 65–72, Ann Arbor, Michigan. Association for Computational Linguistics.

Siqi Bao, Huang He, Fan Wang, Hua Wu, and Haifeng Wang. 2020. PLATO: Pre-trained dialogue generation model with discrete latent variable. In *Proceedings of the 58th Annual Meeting of the Association for Computational Linguistics*, pages 85–96, Online. Association for Computational Linguistics.

Kyunghyun Cho, Bart van Merriënboer, Caglar Gulcehre, Dzmitry Bahdanau, Fethi Bougares, Holger Schwenk, and Yoshua Bengio. 2014. Learning phrase representations using RNN encoder–decoder for statistical machine translation. In *Proceedings of the 2014 Conference on Empirical Methods in Natural Language Processing (EMNLP)*, pages 1724–1734, Doha, Qatar. Association for Computational Linguistics.

Jan Deriu, Alvaro Rodrigo, Arantxa Otegi, Guillermo Echegoyen, Sophie Rosset, Eneko Agirre, and Mark Cieliebak. 2021. Survey on evaluation methods for dialogue systems. *Artificial Intelligence Review*, 54(1):755–810.

Jan Deriu, Don Tuggener, Pius von Däniken, Jon Ander Campos, Alvaro Rodrigo, Thiziri Belkacem, Aitor Soroa, Eneko Agirre, and Mark Cieliebak. 2020. Spot the bot: A robust and efficient framework for the evaluation of conversational dialogue systems. In *Proceedings of the 2020 Conference on Empirical Methods in Natural Language Processing (EMNLP)*, pages 3971–3984, Online. Association for Computational Linguistics.

Jacob Devlin, Ming-Wei Chang, Kenton Lee, and Kristina Toutanova. 2019. BERT: Pre-training of deep bidirectional transformers for language understanding. In *Proceedings of the 2019 Conference of the North American Chapter of the Association for Computational Linguistics: Human Language Technologies, Volume 1 (Long and Short Papers)*, pages 4171–4186, Minneapolis, Minnesota. Association for Computational Linguistics.

Emily Dinan, Varvara Logacheva, Valentin Malykh, Alexander Miller, Kurt Shuster, Jack Urbanek, Douwe Kiela, Arthur Szlam, Iulian Serban, Ryan Lowe, et al. 2019. The second conversational intelligence challenge (convai2). *arXiv preprint arXiv:1902.00098*.

Michel Galley, Chris Brockett, Alessandro Sordoni, Yangfeng Ji, Michael Auli, Chris Quirk, Margaret Mitchell, Jianfeng Gao, and Bill Dolan. 2015. deltaBLEU: A discriminative metric for generation tasks with intrinsically diverse targets. In *Proceedings of the 53rd Annual Meeting of the Association for Computational Linguistics and the 7th International Joint Conference on Natural Language Processing (Volume 2: Short Papers)*, pages 445–450, Beijing, China. Association for Computational Linguistics.

Xiang Gao, Yizhe Zhang, Michel Galley, Chris Brockett, and Bill Dolan. 2020. Dialogue response rankingtraining with large-scale human feedback data. In *EMNLP*.

Sarik Ghazarian, Johnny Wei, Aram Galstyan, and Nanyun Peng. 2019. Better automatic evaluation of open-domain dialogue systems with contextualized embeddings. In *Proceedings of the Workshop on Methods for Optimizing and Evaluating Neural Language Generation*, pages 82–89, Minneapolis, Minnesota. Association for Computational Linguistics.

Sarik Ghazarian, Ralph Weischedel, Aram Galstyan, and Nanyun Peng. 2020. Predictive engagement: An efficient metric for automatic evaluation of open-domain dialogue systems. In *Proceedings of the AAAI Conference on Artificial Intelligence*, volume 34, pages 7789–7796.

Karthik Gopalakrishnan, Behnam Hedayatnia, Qinlang Chen, Anna Gottardi, Sanjeev Kwatra, Anu Venkatesh, Raefer Gabriel, and Dilek Hakkani-Tür. 2019. Topical-Chat: Towards Knowledge-Grounded Open-Domain Conversations. In *Proc. Interspeech 2019*, pages 1891–1895.

Jian Guan and Minlie Huang. 2020. UNION: An Unreferenced Metric for Evaluating Open-ended Story Generation. In *Proceedings of the 2020 Conference* on *Empirical Methods in Natural Language Processing (EMNLP)*, pages 9157–9166, Online. Association for Computational Linguistics.

Chulaka Gunasekara, Seokhwan Kim, Luis Fernando D'Haro, Abhinav Rastogi, Yun-Nung Chen, Mihail Eric, Behnam Hedayatnia, Karthik Gopalakrishnan, Yang Liu, Chao-Wei Huang, et al. 2021. Overview of the ninth dialog system technology challenge: Dstc9. *Proceedings of the 9th Dialog System Technology Challenge Workshop in AAAI2021*.

Fenfei Guo, A. Metallinou, Chandra Khatri, Anirudh Raju, Anu Venkatesh, and A. Ram. 2018. Topic-based evaluation for conversational bots. *ArXiv*, abs/1801.03622.

Michael Gutmann and Aapo Hyvärinen. 2010. Noise-contrastive estimation: A new estimation principle for unnormalized statistical models. In *Proceedings of the Thirteenth International Conference on Artificial Intelligence and Statistics*, pages 297–304. JMLR Workshop and Conference Proceedings.

Chiori Hori and Takaaki Hori. 2017. End-to-end conversation modeling track in dstc6. *arXiv:1706.07440*.

Lishan Huang, Zheng Ye, Jinghui Qin, Liang Lin, and Xiaodan Liang. 2020. GRADE: Automatic graph-enhanced coherence metric for evaluating open-domain dialogue systems. In *Proceedings of the 2020 Conference on Empirical Methods in Natural Language Processing (EMNLP)*, pages 9230–9240, Online. Association for Computational Linguistics.

Ryan Kiros, Yukun Zhu, Ruslan Salakhutdinov, Richard S Zemel, Antonio Torralba, Raquel Urtasun, and Sanja Fidler. 2015. Skip-thought vectors. *arXiv preprint arXiv:1506.06726*.

Tian Lan, Xian-Ling Mao, Wei Wei, Xiaoyan Gao, and Heyan Huang. 2020. Pone: A novel automatic evaluation metric for open-domain generative dialogue systems. *ACM Trans. Inf. Syst.*, 39(1).

Jiwei Li, Michel Galley, Chris Brockett, Jianfeng Gao, and Bill Dolan. 2016. A diversity-promoting objective function for neural conversation models. In *Proceedings of the 2016 Conference of the North American Chapter of the Association for Computational Linguistics: Human Language Technologies*, pages 110–119, San Diego, California. Association for Computational Linguistics.

Yanran Li, Hui Su, Xiaoyu Shen, Wenjie Li, Ziqiang Cao, and Shuzi Niu. 2017. DailyDialog: A manually labelled multi-turn dialogue dataset. In *Proceedings of the Eighth International Joint Conference on Natural Language Processing (Volume 1: Long Papers)*, pages 986–995, Taipei, Taiwan. Asian Federation of Natural Language Processing.

Zekang Li, Jinchao Zhang, Zhengcong Fei, Yang Feng, and Jie Zhou. 2021a. Addressing inquiries about history: An efficient and practical framework for evaluating open-domain chatbot consistency. In *Findings of Proceedings of the 59th Annual Meeting of the Association for Computational Linguistics*.

Zekang Li, Jinchao Zhang, Zhengcong Fei, Yang Feng, and Jie Zhou. 2021b. Conversations are not flat: Modeling the intrinsic information flow between dialogue utterances. In *Proceedings of the 59th Annual Meeting of the Association for Computational Linguistics*.

Chin-Yew Lin. 2004. ROUGE: A package for automatic evaluation of summaries. In *Text Summarization Branches Out*, pages 74–81, Barcelona, Spain. Association for Computational Linguistics.

Chia-Wei Liu, Ryan Lowe, Iulian Serban, Mike Noseworthy, Laurent Charlin, and Joelle Pineau. 2016a. How NOT to evaluate your dialogue system: An empirical study of unsupervised evaluation metrics for dialogue response generation. In *Proceedings of the 2016 Conference on Empirical Methods in Natural Language Processing*, pages 2122–2132, Austin, Texas. Association for Computational Linguistics.

Chia-Wei Liu, Ryan Lowe, Iulian V Serban, Michael Noseworthy, Laurent Charlin, and Joelle Pineau. 2016b. How not to evaluate your dialogue system: An empirical study of unsupervised evaluation metrics for dialogue response generation. *arXiv preprint arXiv:1603.08023*.

Yinhan Liu, Myle Ott, Naman Goyal, Jingfei Du, Mandar Joshi, Danqi Chen, Omer Levy, Mike Lewis, Luke Zettlemoyer, and Veselin Stoyanov. 2019. Roberta: A robustly optimized bert pretraining approach. *arXiv preprint arXiv:1907.11692*.

Ryan Lowe, Michael Noseworthy, Iulian Vlad Serban, Nicolas Angelard-Gontier, Yoshua Bengio, and Joelle Pineau. 2017. Towards an automatic Turing test: Learning to evaluate dialogue responses. In *Proceedings of the 55th Annual Meeting of the Association for Computational Linguistics (Volume 1: Long Papers)*, pages 1116–1126, Vancouver, Canada. Association for Computational Linguistics.

Ryan Lowe, Nissan Pow, Iulian Serban, and Joelle Pineau. 2015. The Ubuntu dialogue corpus: A large dataset for research in unstructured multi-turn dialogue systems. In *Proceedings of the 16th Annual Meeting of the Special Interest Group on Discourse and Dialogue*, pages 285–294, Prague, Czech Republic. Association for Computational Linguistics.

Joel Mackenzie, Rodger Benham, Matthias Petri, Johanne R Trippas, J Shane Culpepper, and Alistair Moffat. 2020. Cc-news-en: A large english news corpus. In *Proceedings of the 29th ACM International Conference on Information & Knowledge Management*, pages 3077–3084.

Shikib Mehri and Maxine Eskenazi. 2020a. Unsupervised evaluation of interactive dialog with DialoGPT. In *Proceedings of the 21th Annual Meeting of the Special Interest Group on Discourse and*

Dialogue, pages 225–235, 1st virtual meeting. Association for Computational Linguistics.

Shikib Mehri and Maxine Eskenazi. 2020b. USR: An unsupervised and reference free evaluation metric for dialog generation. In *Proceedings of the 58th Annual Meeting of the Association for Computational Linguistics*, pages 681–707, Online. Association for Computational Linguistics.

Rostislav Nedelchev, Jens Lehmann, and Ricardo Usbeck. 2020. Language model transformers as evaluators for open-domain dialogues. In *Proceedings of the 28th International Conference on Computational Linguistics*, pages 6797–6808, Barcelona, Spain (Online). International Committee on Computational Linguistics.

Jekaterina Novikova, Ondřej Dušek, Amanda Cercas Curry, and Verena Rieser. 2017. Why we need new evaluation metrics for NLG. In *Proceedings of the 2017 Conference on Empirical Methods in Natural Language Processing*, pages 2241–2252, Copenhagen, Denmark. Association for Computational Linguistics.

Bo Pang, Erik Nijkamp, Wenjuan Han, Linqi Zhou, Yixian Liu, and Kewei Tu. 2020. Towards holistic and automatic evaluation of open-domain dialogue generation. In *Proceedings of the 58th Annual Meeting of the Association for Computational Linguistics*, pages 3619–3629, Online. Association for Computational Linguistics.

Kishore Papineni, Salim Roukos, Todd Ward, and Wei-Jing Zhu. 2002. Bleu: a method for automatic evaluation of machine translation. In *Proceedings of the 40th Annual Meeting of the Association for Computational Linguistics*, pages 311–318, Philadelphia, Pennsylvania, USA. Association for Computational Linguistics.

Vitou Phy, Yang Zhao, and Akiko Aizawa. 2020. Deconstruct to reconstruct a configurable evaluation metric for open-domain dialogue systems. In *Proceedings of the 28th International Conference on Computational Linguistics*, pages 4164–4178, Barcelona, Spain (Online). International Committee on Computational Linguistics.

Alec Radford, Jeffrey Wu, Rewon Child, David Luan, Dario Amodei, and Ilya Sutskever. 2019. Language models are unsupervised multitask learners. *OpenAI blog*, 1(8):9.

Colin Raffel, Noam Shazeer, Adam Roberts, Katherine Lee, Sharan Narang, Michael Matena, Yanqi Zhou, Wei Li, and Peter J. Liu. 2020. Exploring the limits of transfer learning with a unified text-to-text transformer. *Journal of Machine Learning Research*, 21(140):1–67.

Hannah Rashkin, Eric Michael Smith, Margaret Li, and Y-Lan Boureau. 2019. Towards empathetic open-domain conversation models: A new benchmark and dataset. In *Proceedings of the 57th Annual Meeting of the Association for Computational Linguistics*, pages 5370–5381, Florence, Italy. Association for Computational Linguistics.

Cl'ement Rebuffel, Thomas Scialom, Laure Soulier, Benjamin Piwowarski, Sylvain Lamprier, Jacopo Staiano, Geoffrey Scoutheeten, and P. Gallinari. 2021. Data-questeval: A referenceless metric for data to text semantic evaluation. *ArXiv*, abs/2104.07555.

Ehud Reiter. 2018. A structured review of the validity of BLEU. *Computational Linguistics*, 44(3):393–401.

Alan Ritter, Colin Cherry, and William B. Dolan. 2011. Data-driven response generation in social media. In *Proceedings of the 2011 Conference on Empirical Methods in Natural Language Processing*, pages 583–593, Edinburgh, Scotland, UK. Association for Computational Linguistics.

Mario Rodríguez-Cantelar, Luis Fernando D'Haro, and Fernando Matía. 2021. Automatic evaluation of non-task oriented dialog systems by using sentence embeddings projections and their dynamics. In *Conversational Dialogue Systems for the Next Decade*, pages 71–84. Springer.

Ananya B. Sai, Akash Kumar Mohankumar, Siddhartha Arora, and Mitesh M. Khapra. 2020. Improving dialog evaluation with a multi-reference adversarial dataset and large scale pretraining. *Transactions of the Association for Computational Linguistics*, 8:810–827.

Thomas Scialom, Paul-Alexis Dray, Patrick Gallinari, Sylvain Lamprier, Benjamin Piwowarski, Jacopo Staiano, and Alex Wang. 2021. Questeval: Summarization asks for fact-based evaluation. *arXiv preprint arXiv:2103.12693*.

Abigail See, Stephen Roller, Douwe Kiela, and Jason Weston. 2019. What makes a good conversation? how controllable attributes affect human judgments. In *Proceedings of the 2019 Conference of the North American Chapter of the Association for Computational Linguistics: Human Language Technologies, Volume 1 (Long and Short Papers)*, pages 1702–1723, Minneapolis, Minnesota. Association for Computational Linguistics.

Thibault Sellam, Dipanjan Das, and Ankur Parikh. 2020. BLEURT: Learning robust metrics for text generation. In *Proceedings of the 58th Annual Meeting of the Association for Computational Linguistics*, pages 7881–7892, Online. Association for Computational Linguistics.

Hiroki Shimanaka, Tomoyuki Kajiwara, and Mamoru Komachi. 2018. RUSE: Regressor using sentence embeddings for automatic machine translation evaluation. In *Proceedings of the Third Conference on Machine Translation: Shared Task Papers*, pages

751–758, Belgium, Brussels. Association for Computational Linguistics.

Koustuv Sinha, Prasanna Parthasarathi, Jasmine Wang, Ryan Lowe, William L. Hamilton, and Joelle Pineau. 2020. Learning an unreferenced metric for online dialogue evaluation. In *Proceedings of the 58th Annual Meeting of the Association for Computational Linguistics*, pages 2430–2441, Online. Association for Computational Linguistics.

Elior Sulem, Omri Abend, and Ari Rappoport. 2018. BLEU is not suitable for the evaluation of text simplification. In *Proceedings of the 2018 Conference on Empirical Methods in Natural Language Processing*, pages 738–744, Brussels, Belgium. Association for Computational Linguistics.

Chongyang Tao, Lili Mou, Dongyan Zhao, and Rui Yan. 2018. Ruber: An unsupervised method for automatic evaluation of open-domain dialog systems. In *Proceedings of the AAAI Conference on Artificial Intelligence*, volume 32.

Ashish Vaswani, Noam Shazeer, Niki Parmar, Jakob Uszkoreit, Llion Jones, Aidan N Gomez, Łukasz Kaiser, and Illia Polosukhin. 2017. Attention is all you need. In *Advances in neural information processing systems*, pages 5998–6008.

Anu Venkatesh, Chandra Khatri, Ashwin Ram, Fenfei Guo, Raefer Gabriel, Ashish Nagar, Rohit Prasad, Ming Cheng, Behnam Hedayatnia, Angeliki Metallinou, et al. 2018. On evaluating and comparing conversational agents. *arXiv preprint arXiv:1801.03625*, 4:60–68.

Marilyn A. Walker, Diane J. Litman, Candace A. Kamm, and Alicia Abella. 1997. PARADISE: A framework for evaluating spoken dialogue agents. In *35th Annual Meeting of the Association for Computational Linguistics and 8th Conference of the European Chapter of the Association for Computational Linguistics*, pages 271–280, Madrid, Spain. Association for Computational Linguistics.

Alex Wang, Amanpreet Singh, Julian Michael, Felix Hill, Omer Levy, and Samuel Bowman. 2018. GLUE: A multi-task benchmark and analysis platform for natural language understanding. In *Proceedings of the 2018 EMNLP Workshop BlackboxNLP: Analyzing and Interpreting Neural Networks for NLP*, pages 353–355, Brussels, Belgium. Association for Computational Linguistics.

Jiannan Xiang, Yahui Liu, Deng Cai, Huayang Li, Defu Lian, and Lemao Liu. 2021. Assessing dialogue systems with distribution distances. *arXiv preprint arXiv:2105.02573*.

Tsuta Yuma, Naoki Yoshinaga, and Masashi Toyoda. 2020. uBLEU: Uncertainty-aware automatic evaluation method for open-domain dialogue systems. In *Proceedings of the 58th Annual Meeting of the Association for Computational Linguistics: Student Research Workshop*, pages 199–206, Online. Association for Computational Linguistics.

Chen Zhang, Yiming Chen, Luis Fernando D'Haro, Yan Zhang, Thomas Friedrichs, Grandee Lee, and Haizhou Li. 2021a. Dynaeval: Unifying turn and dialogue level evaluation. In *The Joint Conference of the 59th Annual Meeting of the Association for Computational Linguistics and the 11th International Joint Conference on Natural Language Processing (ACL-IJCNLP 2021)*, Online.

Chen Zhang, Luis Fernando D'Haro, Rafael E Banchs, Thomas Friedrichs, and Haizhou Li. 2021b. Deep am-fm: Toolkit for automatic dialogue evaluation. In *Conversational Dialogue Systems for the Next Decade*, pages 53–69. Springer.

Saizheng Zhang, Emily Dinan, Jack Urbanek, Arthur Szlam, Douwe Kiela, and Jason Weston. 2018. Personalizing dialogue agents: I have a dog, do you have pets too? In *Proceedings of the 56th Annual Meeting of the Association for Computational Linguistics (Volume 1: Long Papers)*, pages 2204–2213, Melbourne, Australia. Association for Computational Linguistics.

Tianyi Zhang, Varsha Kishore, Felix Wu, Kilian Q Weinberger, and Yoav Artzi. 2019. Bertscore: Evaluating text generation with bert. *arXiv preprint arXiv:1904.09675*.

Yizhe Zhang, Siqi Sun, Michel Galley, Yen-Chun Chen, Chris Brockett, Xiang Gao, Jianfeng Gao, Jingjing Liu, and Bill Dolan. 2020. Dialogpt: Large-scale generative pre-training for conversational response generation. In *ACL, system demonstration*.

Tiancheng Zhao, Ran Zhao, and Maxine Eskenazi. 2017a. Learning discourse-level diversity for neural dialog models using conditional variational autoencoders. In *Proceedings of the 55th Annual Meeting of the Association for Computational Linguistics (Volume 1: Long Papers)*, pages 654–664, Vancouver, Canada. Association for Computational Linguistics.

Tiancheng Zhao, Ran Zhao, and Maxine Eskenazi. 2017b. Learning discourse-level diversity for neural dialog models using conditional variational autoencoders. *arXiv preprint arXiv:1703.10960*.

Wangchunshu Zhou and Ke Xu. 2020. Learning to compare for better training and evaluation of open domain natural language generation models. In *Proceedings of the AAAI Conference on Artificial Intelligence*, volume 34, pages 9717–9724.

Yukun Zhu, Ryan Kiros, Rich Zemel, Ruslan Salakhutdinov, Raquel Urtasun, Antonio Torralba, and Sanja Fidler. 2015. Aligning books and movies: Towards story-like visual explanations by watching movies and reading books. In *Proceedings of the IEEE international conference on computer vision*, pages 19–27.

A Details of Studied Automatic Metrics

A.1 Design of the Metrics in this Assessment

In general, dialog evaluation metrics can be divided into rule-based and model-based metrics. Rule-based metrics use heuristic rules to evaluate the system response, conditioned on the dialog context and human reference(s). Model-based metrics are trained, often with self-supervised objectives, to measure the quality of the responses.

BLEU (Papineni et al., 2002) is a popular rule-based metric often used to benchmark natural language generation (NLG) systems. BLEU computes the n-gram precision of the system responses using human references. While BLEU performs reasonably when evaluating NLG systems, it has issues reflecting grammaticality, use of semantically similar words, and meaning preservation (Novikova et al., 2017; Ananthakrishnan et al., 2007; Sulem et al., 2018; Reiter, 2018).

METEOR (Banerjee and Lavie, 2005) and ROUGE (Lin, 2004) have been proposed to address the shortcomings of BLEU. METEOR incorporates stems and synonyms into its calculation, while ROUGE focuses on n-gram recall instead of precision. Although these two metrics improve upon BLEU, they remain ineffective for dialog evaluation (Liu et al., 2016b). In general, word-overlap metrics struggle to evaluate dialog responses because of the one-to-many nature of dialog (Zhao et al., 2017b). Concretely, as mentioned above, since there are many appropriate responses for a given dialog context it is unreasonable to penalize a valid system response that deviates from the ground truth.

ADEM (Lowe et al., 2017) is an early learning-based metric that uses a recurrent neural network (RNN) to predict the quality of system responses. ADEM uses quality-annotated training data and the model is trained to predict human quality annotations with a mean squared error loss (MSE).

RUBER (Tao et al., 2018) uses a hybrid model consisting of both a referenced metric and an unreferenced metric. The referenced metric calculates the cosine similarity of word embeddings between a system response and a human reference. The unreferenced metric is trained with a triplet ranking loss to predict whether the generated response is appropriate for the dialog history. BERT-RUBER (Ghazarian et al., 2019) proposes to replace the RNN in RUBER with BERT (Devlin et al., 2019) to further improve the performance with contextualized word embeddings.

Based on BERT-RUBER, PONE (Lan et al., 2020) uses a novel algorithm to sample negative examples during training, and trains the metric on a dataset augmented by other NLG models.

MAUDE (Sinha et al., 2020) is trained with Noise Contrastive Estimation (NCE) (Gutmann and Hyvärinen, 2010) which requires the model to differentiate between a correct response and randomly sampled negative responses.

DEB (Sai et al., 2020) constructs a dialog dataset which consists of manually-created relevant responses and adversarial irrelevant responses. DEB uses BERT for dialog evaluation by first pretraining on a large-scale dialog corpus, and then fine-tuning on the proposed dataset with a next sentence prediction (NSP) objective.

GRADE (Huang et al., 2020) models topic transition dynamics in dialog by constructing a graph representation of the dialog history. This graph is then passed as input to a model that is trained with the same triplet loss as RUBER.

While GRADE is focused on turn-level topic transition dynamics in dialog, DynaEval (Zhang et al., 2021a) leverages a graph structure to model the dialog-level interactions between a user and a system. Through this graph-based approach, DynaEval is trained to distinguish well-formed dialogs from carefully constructed negative samples.

USR (Mehri and Eskenazi, 2020b) trains several models to measure different qualities of dialogs. USR relies on three different models, (1) a language model, trained with the masked language modelling (MLM) objectives, measures fluency, (2) a dialog retrieval model determines the relevance of a response and (3) a fact-to-response selection model measures whether a response conditions on knowledge.

Similarly, USL-H (Phy et al., 2020) combines three models trained with different objectives: valid utterance prediction (VUP), next sentence prediction (NSP), and MLM. The VUP model determines whether a response is valid and grammatically correct. The NSP model and MLM models are trained with self-supervised objectives to evaluate the sensibleness and the likelihood of a given response.

DialogRPT (Gao et al., 2020) is an ensemble of multiple GPT-2 based models, which were fine-tuned on the Reddit human feedback data with different tasks. The tasks include predicting human feedback of responses and whether the response is

Metrics	Reason for not using
UNION (2020)	Designed for story generation
Embedding Methods (2015; 2016a; 2021)	Computing the embedding similarity is identical to the referenced metric in RUBER.
Language Model Evaluator (2020)	Using the language model probability is identical to the approach of USR and HolisticEval.
Perplexity (2020a)	No access to the NLG models that generated the quality-annotated data in order to obtain perplexity.
Distinct N-grams (2016)	This is not feasible for models trained on dialog corpora (Pang et al., 2020).
Spot The Bot (2020)	This still needs human annotation when evaluating models.
Learning to Compare (2020)	No released code, data, or pretrained models.
RUSE (2018)	Designed for machine translation only.
uBLEU (2020)	No released code.
deltaBLEU (2015)	For each response, this requires multiple human references to calculate the score.
Data-QuestEval (2021)	Designed for general NLU, not specifically for dialog.
Topic-based Evaluation (2018)	No released code, data, or pretrained models.
The Alexa Prize Evaluation Framework (2018)	No released code, data, or pretrained models.
AIH (2021a)	No released code, data, or pretrained models.

Table 5: The metrics that were not assessed in this paper and the reasons behind that choice.

human-like.

The Deep AM-FM metric (Zhang et al., 2021b) measures two aspects of dialog quality through the Adequacy Metric (AM) and the Fluency Metric (FM). AM assesses the semantic similarity of system responses and human references by comparing their BERT embeddings. FM compares the similarity of the language model probabilities for both the system response and the human reference, and produces a higher score if the probabilities are similar.

HolisticEval (Pang et al., 2020) evaluates several qualities of dialog: *context coherence*, *language fluency*, *response diversity*, and *logical self-consistency*. The GPT-2 language model (Radford et al., 2019) and pretrained Natural Language Inference models are used to measure these qualities.

In addition to measuring the relevance of a response, PredictiveEngage (Ghazarian et al., 2020) incorporates an utterance-level engagement classifier to better assess the overall quality of a response.

FED (Mehri and Eskenazi, 2020a) is an unsupervised evaluation metric that uses DialoGPT (Zhang et al., 2020) to measure 18 fine-grained qualities of dialog. FED calculates the likelihood of manually designed follow-up utterances to measure multiple qualities of dialog without any supervision.

FlowScore (Li et al., 2021b) which is based on the DialoFlow model, models the dynamic information flow in the dialog history to evaluate the quality of a dialog. DialoFlow is a response generation model that is trained with three objectives CFM, SIM and RGM in order to condition the response generation on the context flow in the dialog. FlowScore uses the representations produced by DialoFlow to measure the dialog quality.

FBD (Xiang et al., 2021) computes the distribution-wise difference between the system generated conversations and the human-written conversations to evaluate the performance of a dialog system. FBD focuses on assessing system-level performance and leverages the pretrained RoBERTa model without any additional fine-tuning.

In addition to automatic metrics specifically designed for dialog evaluation, this paper also evaluates the performance of BERTScore (Zhang et al., 2019), QuestEval (Scialom et al., 2021), and BLEURT (Sellam et al., 2020) which were originally designed for evaluating machine translation, summarization and general natural language generation. BERTScore computes the F1 score by matching token embeddings in the human reference and system response. BLEURT generates synthetic data to pre-train BERT and fine-tune the model to predict a human score with MSE loss. QuestEval, which is based on question generation (QG) and question answering (QA), accounts for factual consistency, relevance, and information selection of the generated response. While these three metrics were not specifically designed for dialog, it is interesting to observe how they perform on dialog data.

A.2 Use of Pretrained Language Models

Large-scale pretrained language models (Devlin et al., 2019; Radford et al., 2019) have been ubiquitous in NLP models. Embeddings from pretrained language models have been shown to be particularly effective for a variety of NLP tasks. Pretrained models are now a commonly-used strategy in dialog evaluation metrics. However, since different pretrained models use different training data and objectives, the choice of language model might significantly influence the final performance and generalizability of the evaluation metrics. *Future work should explore the impact of the different pretrained language models on the performance of the evaluation metric.*

BERT (Devlin et al., 2019) is used in many of

the metrics that this paper assesses. BERT uses the Masked Language Modeling (MLM) and Next Sentence Prediction (NSP) objectives, and is trained on the BookCorpus (Zhu et al., 2015) and English Wikipedia.

RoBERTa, which is employed in USR (Mehri and Eskenazi, 2020b), improves the training techniques in BERT and trains the model on a much larger corpus which includes the CommonCrawl News dataset (Mackenzie et al., 2020) and text extracted from Reddit. Specifically, the full training data size of RoBERTa is 10 times larger than BERT, and empirically RoBERTa has better performance than BERT on common NLP tasks including the GLUE benchmark (Wang et al., 2018).

FED (Mehri and Eskenazi, 2020a) uses DialoGPT (Zhang et al., 2020) which is based on the GPT2 (Radford et al., 2019) architecture and trained with dialog data extracted from Reddit. Due to this, DialoGPT might better model human conversation, particularly open-domain chit-chat.

Deep AM-FM uses Multilingual BERT (Devlin et al., 2019), which is BERT trained on multilingual datasets. *The benefits of using multilingual language models to evaluate English data is unclear and is an interesting topic for future work.*

T5 (Raffel et al., 2020), which is used by QuestEval, is a Transformer Seq2Seq model pretrained on a massive text corpus. T5 achieved state-of-the-art results on many text generation tasks including summarization, question answering, and text classification. The strong performance of T5 on NLG tasks, suggests that it may be valuable in the assessment of response generation models.

A.3 Training Data

The choice of training data is one of the most important factors in model-based metrics. The domain, quality, and conversation setting of the dataset all play important roles in the relative quality of the resulting metric. For example, a metric trained on Twitter data may also perform well at evaluating dialogs generated for Reddit data, since the two datasets are constructed from online forums. This section introduces the characteristics of the datasets used to train the various model-based metrics.

DailyDialog (Li et al., 2017) is a human-written dialog dataset where the conversation topics are about day-to-day life.

PersonaChat (Zhang et al., 2018) is a dataset that consists of persona-conditioned dialogs where each participant is assigned a persona and the goal is to become familiar with the other individual. In contrast to DailyDialog, dialogs in PersonaChat have a clear objective and are more engaging.

The ConvAI dataset (Dinan et al., 2019) is based on PersonaChat with modifications to preprocessing and additional training examples.

TopicalChat (Gopalakrishnan et al., 2019) consists of knowledge-grounded human-human conversations, wherein two individuals have a conversation grounded on 'interesting facts'. Models trained on TopicalChat are expected to be able to use external knowledge and have realistic knowledge-grounded conversations.

Twitter (Ritter et al., 2011) and Ubuntu Dialogue (Lowe et al., 2015) both result from a crawl of the internet. Ubuntu Dialogue has very technical conversations regarding computer systems, while Twitter covers a broad, general set of topics.

These datasets were generally used to train the metrics through the use of self-supervised objectives.

A.4 Referenced vs Reference-Free

Word-overlap metrics are ineffective for dialog (Liu et al., 2016b) largely due to the one-to-many nature of dialog (Zhao et al., 2017a). While this could be mitigated by using multiple reference responses, it is infeasible to collect a sufficiently large dataset to thoroughly cover the space of potential responses. Thus, reference-free metrics have been proposed to circumvent the one-to-many problem. Amongst the metrics assessed here, there are several reference-free evaluation metrics: HolisticEval, MAUDE, GRADE, USR, FED, FlowSore, USL-H, QuestEval, DEB, DynaEval, PredictiveEngage and DialogRPT.

In contrast to the referenced metrics, which compare the generated response to the reference response, reference-free metrics model the semantics of the dialog context and the generated response in order to reason about the response within the context of the dialog history.

A.5 Metrics not Assessed in this Paper

Table 5 lists recently proposed dialog metrics that are not assessed in this paper. There are several reasons a metric was not assessed:

- The metric was not designed specifically for dialog. While most of these metrics were not included, a few metrics that fall into this

category (e.g., BERTScore, QuestEval, and BLEURT) were assessed here, as a baseline and to represent this category.
- There was no released code, data, or pre-trained model for reproducing their results.
- The core idea of the metric is very similar to metrics that were assessed.
- The metric is infeasible to assess in our experimental setting, as it requires additional annotations. This may include requiring human annotations or information about the response generation models.

Some of the unassessed metrics that share ideas that are covered by other metrics assessed in this paper are:

Embedding Methods (Kiros et al., 2015; Liu et al., 2016a; Rodríguez-Cantelar et al., 2021) compute the similarity of system responses with the human reference through embeddings, which is equivalent to the approach used by RUBER and BERTScore.

Language Model Evaluator (Nedelchev et al., 2020) evaluates dialog using the language model likelihood, which is identical to the approaches of USR and HolisticEval.

B Testing Datasets

B.1 Data Collection

This section provides an overview of the different quality-annotated dialog datasets. Many of these datasets were collected in different settings. For example, as described in Section A.3, DailyDialog consists of casual conversations about daily life while TopicalChat consists of knowledge-grounded conversations. These differences influence various aspects of the data, such as the formality and complexity of the sentence structure. However, since it is not easy to quantify the complexity of the sentence structure, the average length and the number of distinct words in the dialog context (Ctx), human reference (Ref) and model hypothesis (Hyp) are used in Table 6. The length of the context and reference response in DailyDialog is shorter than on TopicalChat, which is likely influenced by the simpler topics in DailyDialog.

GRADE-DailyDialog has a significantly longer dialog history than the other two quality-annotated datasets that use DailyDialog. This is because those two datasets, HolisticEval and PredictiveEngage, only use one utterance of the dialog while GRADE uses two utterances. On the other hand, responses in PredictiveEngage-DailyDialog use a larger number of distinct words, which is due to the fact that PredictiveEngage-DailyDialog also contains human-written responses in addition to responses generated by NLG systems.

While most of the dialog data was collected by recruiting human annotators via Amazon Mechanical Turks (AMT), the DSTC6 data (Hori and Hori, 2017) uses dialogs from Twitter. Therefore, we can expect the DSTC6 data to be noisier and more realistic. It poses a challenge for both NLG models and evaluation metrics.

In contrast to other quality-annotated datasets in which the dialog contexts are conversations between humans and only the responses are generated by the system, the DSTC9 and FED datasets provide human-system dialogs that were collected in an interactive setting. The DSTC9 data (Gunasekara et al., 2021) was collected on the DialPort platform through direct interaction between real users and open-domain chit-chat systems. The FED data (Mehri and Eskenazi, 2020a) contains both human-human and human-system conversations released by Adiwardana et al. (2020b).

Despite using the same underlying dialog dataset (e.g., DailyDialog), the complexity and quality of the response may differ significantly across the quality-annotated datasets depending on the response generation model that was used. If responses in a quality-annotated dataset are from both simple sequence-to-sequence (Seq2Seq) models (Cho et al., 2014) and state-of-the-art language models such as DialoGPT, this quality-annotated dataset can assess whether the metric can distinguish between high quality and low quality responses.

Distinguishing between responses produced by systems of very different quality is easier, since the low quality responses may not follow grammar rules and make simple mistakes. On the other hand, if responses are only generated by state-of-the-art systems, the task becomes harder because the metric needs to rank responses as to whether they are appropriate in a dialog context.

Responses in USR-TopicalChat, USR-PersonaChat, HolisticEval-DailyDialog and the DSTC6 data are generated by a relatively simple model, such as an LSTM language model (LSTM LM), LSTM or Transformer Seq2Seq model, or Memory Network.

Dataset	Num. Samples	Avg. Utts.	Avg. Ctx/Ref/Hyp Words	Distinct Ctx/Ref/Hyp Words	Used NLG models
USR-TopicalChat	300	12.2	236.3 / 25.3 / 22.4	2379 / 571 / 1018	Trans
USR-PersonaChat	240	9.3	98.4 / 11.7 / 12.1	1320 / 291 / 609	Trans Seq2Seq, LSTM LM, Memory Network
GRADE-ConvAI2	600	2.0	23.4 / 12.1 / 11.3	1342 / 841 / 1100	Trans Seq2Seq, DialoGPT, BERT/Trans Ranker
GRADE-DailyDialog	300	2.0	24.5 / 12.9 / 10.8	1126 / 674 / 796	Trans Seq2Seq, Trans Ranker
HolisticEval-DailyDialog	200	1.0	14.3 / - / 14.7	847 / - / 875	LSTM Seq2Seq
PredictiveEngage-DailyDialog	600	1.0	12.0 / - / 13.7	1022 / - / 2475	LSTM Seq2Seq
GRADE-ED (2019)	300	2.0	28.0 / 17.8 / 15.6	1430 / 1098 / 701	Trans Seq2Seq, Trans Ranker
DSTC6 (2017)	40000	1.6	30.7 / 19.0 / 19.8	7399 / 3410 / 2473	Systems based on LSTM Seq2Seq
FED (2020a)	500	11.8	86.5 / - / 11.8	3628 / - / 1859	Meena, Mitsuku
DSTC9 (2021)	2200	27.2	231.7 / - / 10.6	35591 / - / 4839	SOTA systems including Plato and DialoGPT

Table 6: Statistics of quality-annotated datasets. Ctx, Ref, and Hyp indicate dialog context, human reference, and model hypothesis, respectively. Trans and ED are the abbreviation of the Transformer and EmpatheticDialogue respectively.

On the other hand, responses in the quality-annotated data labeled by GRADE come from the Transformer Seq2Seq model, DialoGPT, and retrieval model using Transformer or BERT (Transformer/BERT Ranker), which have relatively better empirical performance. Furthermore, FED and DSTC9 data use state-of-the-art dialog systems to generate responses. Specifically, FED data incorporates two systems, Meena (Adiwardana et al., 2020b) and Mitsuku[2], and the DSTC9 data uses dialog systems including PLATO (Bao et al., 2020). These high quality responses make the data more challenging.

B.2 Quality Annotation

After generating responses for each dataset, human annotators labeled the quality of each response. While most quality-annotated datasets provide annotations for the overall score of a given response, HolisticEval-DailyDialog only labels the context coherence of a response.[3]. In addition to the overall score, USR and FED data provide annotations for different dialog qualities such as whether the response is coherent or interesting. These fine-grained annotations allow for a more comprehensive analysis of metrics.

C Experiments

C.1 Metric Output Similarities

To analyze the similarities between the metrics, we plot the correlation between metric outputs in Figure 3. As expected, there is a strong correlation between the outputs of BERTSCore, and BLEURT, the rule-based metrics. Interestingly, Deep AM-FM also is strongly correlated with these word-overlap metrics. This is surprising since Deep AM-FM was specifically designed for evaluating dialog while the others are intended for general-purpose NLG evaluation. This may be because the Deep AM-FM metric compares the generated response to the reference response and, as such, will favor generated responses that have high word-overlap with the reference response.

BERT-RUBER, PONE, GRADE, and USL-H are another group of metrics with similar behavior. Since BERT-RUBER, PONE, and GRADE share a common triplet rank loss and train on DailyDialog, it is not surprising that these three metrics behave similarly. Although USL-H is trained with different objectives, the same behavior might be due to the use of the same training data (DailyDialog) and the same pretrained model (BERT). Moreover, USR has a slightly higher correlation to this group. This is likely because USR aggregates multiple qualities similar to USL-H and models the relevance of responses, similar to the RUBER-based metrics and GRADE.

C.2 Performance on Different Response Generation Models

This section presents the correlations of the metrics on both generative and retrieval response generation models (see Table 10). Most of the metrics perform similarly on these two types of models. However, USR, GRADE, and FlowScore perform very differently. USR and GRADE are especially good at scoring responses from the retrieval model. USR performs significantly less well at evaluating generative models while GRADE still achieves the highest correlation. In contrast, FlowScore performs well at evaluating generative models but performs poorly on generative models. One reason for this may be that responses from generative models are longer and more complex than the ones from retrieval models.

[2] https://medium.com/pandorabots-blog/mitsuku-wins-loebner-prize-2018-3e8d98c5f2a7

[3] HolisticEval also released the data for evaluating response fluency. However since the data does not clearly disambiguate between the dialog context and the corresponding system response, it was not used in this paper

	USR-TopicalChat				USR-PersonaChat			
	Turn-Level		System-Level		Turn-Level		System-Level	
	P	S	P	S	P	S	P	S
BLEU-4	0.216	0.296	0.874*	0.900	0.135	0.090*	0.841*	0.800*
METEOR	0.336	0.391	0.943	0.900	0.253	0.271	0.907*	0.800*
ROUGE-L	0.275	0.287	0.814*	0.900	0.066*	0.038*	0.171*	0.000*
ADEM	-0.060*	-0.061*	0.202*	0.700*	-0.141	-0.085*	0.523*	0.400*
BERTScore	0.298	0.325	0.854*	0.900	0.152	0.122*	0.241*	0.000*
BLEURT	0.216	0.261	0.630*	0.900	0.065*	0.054*	-0.125*	0.000*
QuestEval	0.300	0.338	0.943	**1.000**	0.176	0.236	0.885*	**1.000**
RUBER	0.247	0.259	0.876*	**1.000**	0.131	0.190	**0.997**	**1.000**
BERT-RUBER	0.342	0.348	**0.992**	0.900	0.266	0.248	0.958	0.200*
PONE	0.271	0.274	0.893	0.500*	0.373	0.375	0.979	0.800*
MAUDE	0.044*	0.083*	0.317*	-0.200*	0.345	0.298	0.440*	0.400*
DEB	0.180	0.116	0.818*	0.400*	0.291	0.373	0.989	**1.000**
GRADE	0.200	0.217	0.553*	0.100*	0.358	0.352	0.811*	**1.000**
DynaEval	-0.032*	-0.022*	-0.248*	0.100*	0.149	0.171	0.584*	0.800*
USR	**0.412**	**0.423**	0.967	0.900	0.440	0.418	0.864*	**1.000**
USL-H	0.322	0.340	0.966	0.900	**0.495**	**0.523**	0.969	0.800*
DialogRPT	0.120	0.105*	0.944	0.600*	-0.064*	-0.083*	0.347*	0.800*
Deep AM-FM	0.285	0.268	0.969	0.700*	0.228	0.219	0.965	**1.000**
HolisticEval	-0.147	-0.123	-0.919	-0.200*	0.087*	0.113*	0.051*	0.000*
PredictiveEngage	0.222	0.310	0.870*	0.900	-0.003*	0.033*	0.683*	0.200*
FED	-0.124	-0.135	0.730*	0.100*	-0.028*	-0.000*	0.005*	0.400*
FlowScore	0.095*	0.082*	-0.150*	0.400*	0.118*	0.079*	0.678*	0.800*
FBD	-	-	0.916	0.100*	-	-	0.644*	0.800*

Table 7: Results on the USR data. All values are statistically significant to $p < 0.05$, unless marked by *.

	GRADE-ConvAI2				GRADE-DailyDialog				GRADE-EmpatheticDialogue			
	Turn-Level		System-Level		Turn-Level		System-Level		Turn-Level		System-Level	
	P	S	P	S	P	S	P	S	P	S	P	S
BLEU-4	0.003*	0.128	0.034*	0.000*	0.075*	0.184	**1.000***	**1.000**	-0.051*	0.002*	**1.000***	**1.000**
METEOR	0.145	0.181	0.781*	0.600*	0.096*	0.010*	-1.000*	-1.000	0.118	0.055*	**1.000***	**1.000**
ROUGE-L	0.136	0.140	0.209*	0.000*	0.154	0.147	**1.000***	**1.000**	0.029*	-0.013*	**1.000***	**1.000**
ADEM	-0.060*	-0.057*	-0.368*	-0.200*	0.064*	0.071*	**1.000***	**1.000**	-0.036*	-0.028*	**1.000***	**1.000**
BERTScore	0.225	0.224	0.918*	0.800*	0.129	0.100*	-1.000*	-1.000	0.046*	0.033*	**1.000***	**1.000**
BLEURT	0.125	0.120	-0.777*	-0.400*	0.176	0.133	**1.000***	**1.000**	0.087*	0.051*	**1.000***	**1.000**
QuestEval	0.279	0.319	0.283*	0.400*	0.020*	0.006*	-1.000*	-1.000	0.201	0.272	**1.000***	**1.000**
RUBER	-0.027*	-0.042*	-0.458*	-0.400*	-0.084*	-0.094*	-1.000*	-1.000	-0.078*	-0.039*	**1.000***	**1.000**
BERT-RUBER	0.309	0.314	0.885*	**1.000**	0.134	0.128	-1.000*	-1.000	0.163	0.148	**1.000***	**1.000**
PONE	0.362	0.373	0.816*	0.800*	0.163	0.163	-1.000*	-1.000	0.177	0.161	**1.000***	**1.000**
MAUDE	0.351	0.304	0.748*	0.800*	-0.036*	-0.073*	**1.000***	**1.000**	0.007*	-0.057*	**1.000***	**1.000**
DEB	0.426	0.504	**0.995**	**1.000**	**0.337**	**0.363**	1.000*	1.000	**0.356**	**0.395**	**1.000***	**1.000**
GRADE	**0.566**	**0.571**	0.883*	0.800*	0.278	0.253	-1.000*	-1.000	0.330	0.297	**1.000***	**1.000**
DynaEval	0.138	0.131	-0.996	-1.000	0.108*	0.120	-1.000*	-1.000	0.146	0.141	-1.000*	-1.000
USR	0.501	0.500	**0.995**	**1.000**	0.057*	0.057*	-1.000*	-1.000	0.264	0.255	**1.000***	**1.000**
USL-H	0.443	0.457	0.971	1.000	0.108*	0.093*	-1.000*	-1.000	0.293	0.235	**1.000***	**1.000**
DialogRPT	0.137	0.158	-0.311*	-0.600*	-0.000*	0.037*	-1.000*	-1.000	0.211	0.203	1.000*	1.000
Deep AM-FM	0.117	0.130	0.774*	0.400*	0.026*	0.022*	**1.000***	**1.000**	0.083*	0.058*	**1.000***	**1.000**
HolisticEval	-0.030*	-0.010*	-0.297*	-0.400*	0.025*	0.020*	**1.000***	**1.000**	0.199	0.204	-1.000*	-1.000
PredictiveEngage	0.154	0.164	0.601*	0.600*	-0.133	-0.135	-1.000*	-1.000	-0.032*	-0.078*	**1.000***	**1.000**
FED	-0.090	-0.072*	-0.254*	0.000*	0.080*	0.064*	**1.000***	**1.000**	-0.014*	-0.044*	**1.000***	**1.000**
FlowScore	-	-	-	-	-	-	-	-	-	-	-	-
FBD	-	-	-0.235*	-0.400*	-	-	-1.000*	-1.000	-	-	-1.000*	-1.000

Table 8: Results on the GRADE data. All values are statistically significant to $p < 0.05$, unless marked by *.

	DSTC6			
	Turn-Level		System-Level	
	P	S	P	S
BLEU-4	0.131	0.298	-0.064*	0.050*
METEOR	0.307	0.323	0.633	0.084*
ROUGE-L	0.332	0.326	0.487	0.215*
ADEM	0.151	0.118	0.042*	0.347*
BERTScore	**0.369**	**0.337**	0.671	0.265*
BLEURT	0.326	0.294	0.213*	0.426*
QuestEval	0.188	0.242	-0.215*	0.206*
RUBER	0.114	0.092	-0.074*	0.104*
BERT-RUBER	0.204	0.217	**0.825**	0.093*
PONE	0.208	0.200	0.608	0.235*
MAUDE	0.195	0.128	0.739	0.217*
DEB	0.211	0.214	-0.261*	0.492
GRADE	0.119	0.122	0.784	0.611
DynaEval	0.286	0.246	0.342*	-0.050*
USR	0.184	0.166	0.432*	0.147*
USL-H	0.217	0.179	0.811	0.298*
DialogRPT	0.170	0.155	0.567	0.334*
Deep AM-FM	0.326	0.295	0.817	**0.674**
HolisticEval	0.001*	-0.004*	0.010	-0.002
PredictiveEngage	0.043	0.004*	-0.094*	-0.409*
FED	-0.106	-0.083	0.221*	0.322*
FlowScore	0.064	0.095	0.352*	0.362*
FBD	-	-	-0.481	-0.234*

Table 9: Results on the DSTC6 data. All values are statistically significant to $p < 0.05$, unless marked by *.

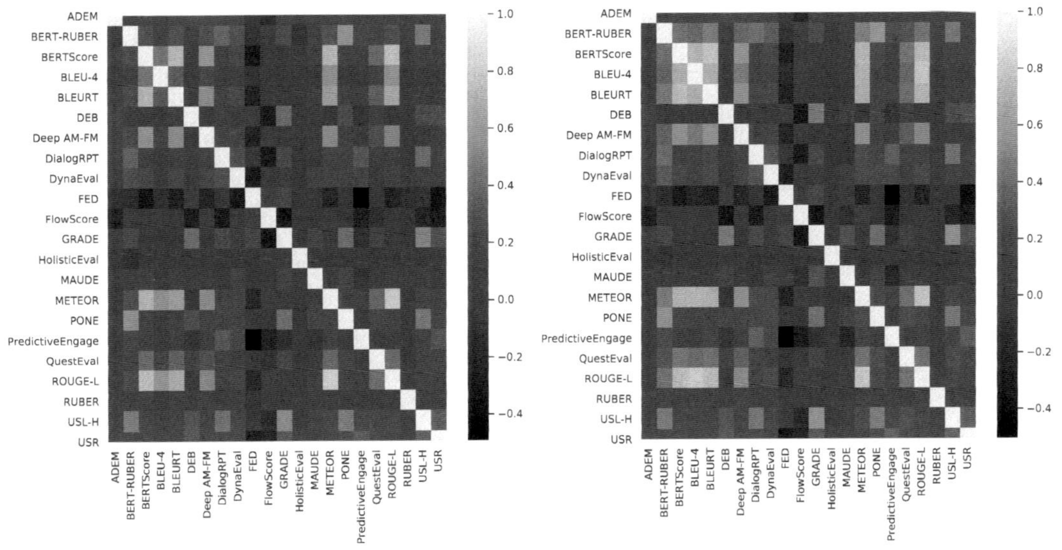

(a) Pearson

(b) Spearman

Figure 3: Pearson and Spearman correlation between different system outputs. We use datasets with human references to compute scores.

	Generative		Retrieval	
	P	S	P	S
BLEU-4	0.100	0.128	0.023*	0.236
METEOR	0.130	0.086	0.129	0.185
ROUGE-L	0.134	0.108	0.212	0.238
ADEM	-0.117	-0.118	-0.045*	-0.070*
BERTScore	0.182	0.185	0.175	0.186
BLEURT	0.153	0.147	0.108	0.093
QuestEval	0.115	0.112	0.105	0.190
RUBER	0.022*	0.031*	-0.092	-0.109
BERT-RUBER	0.158	0.159	0.206	0.208
PONE	0.227	0.236	0.191	0.192
MAUDE	0.126	0.161	0.072*	0.031*
DEB	0.281	0.313	0.307	0.420
GRADE	**0.300**	**0.314**	**0.435**	**0.428**
DynaEval	0.110	0.113	0.143	0.157
USR	0.130	0.149	0.402	0.415
USL-H	0.126	0.161	0.307	0.330
DialogRPT	-0.082	-0.067	-0.009*	0.001*
Deep AM-FM	0.068	0.068	0.086	0.085
HolisticEval	-0.037*	-0.003*	0.070*	0.066*
PredictiveEngage	-0.063*	-0.060*	0.010*	0.028*
FED	-0.072	-0.095	-0.169	-0.184
FlowScore	0.236	0.215	-0.059*	-0.053*
FBD	-	-	-	-

Table 10: Results on evaluating different response generation models. All values are statistically significant to $p < 0.05$, unless marked by *.

	USR-TopicalChat		USR-PersonaChat		GRADE-ConvAI2		GRADE-DailyDialog		GRADE-EmpatheticDialogue		DSTC6	
	P	S	P	S	P	S	P	S	P	S	P	S
PredictiveEngage	0.222	0.310	-0.003*	0.033*	0.154	0.164	-0.133	-0.135	-0.032*	-0.078*	0.043	0.004*
+ RUBER	0.283	0.327	0.057*	0.096*	0.105	0.102	-0.149	-0.156	-0.065*	-0.055*	0.103	0.055
+ PONE	0.308	0.350	0.218	0.209	0.333	0.339	-0.034*	-0.035*	0.077*	0.069*	0.156	0.122
USR	0.412	0.423	0.440	0.418	0.501	0.500	0.057*	0.057*	0.264	0.255	0.184	0.166
+ GRADE	0.424	0.432	0.456	0.430	0.523	0.528	0.081*	0.078*	0.281	0.267	0.191	0.173
+ USL-H	0.429	0.440	0.468	0.451	0.517	0.522	0.062*	0.062*	0.278	0.265	0.197	0.178
+ DEB	0.359	0.362	0.453	0.473	0.552	0.551	0.222	0.190	0.391	0.385	0.248	0.234
+ GRADE + PONE	0.435	0.447	0.473	0.452	0.535	0.539	0.089	0.086	0.289	0.270	0.206	0.187
+ GRADE + PONE + PE	0.447	0.468	0.468	0.449	0.534	0.538	0.072*	0.070*	0.275	0.261	0.202	0.180
+ GRADE + USL-H + DEB	0.377	0.382	0.476	0.495	**0.571**	**0.579**	0.229	0.198	**0.399**	0.387	0.254	0.238
GRADE	0.200	0.217	0.358	0.352	0.566	0.571	0.278	0.253	0.330	0.297	0.119	0.122
+ PONE	0.282	0.297	0.435	0.436	0.547	0.556	0.275	0.279	0.306	0.279	0.191	0.179
+ PONE + PE	0.335	0.348	0.373	0.366	0.515	0.530	0.118	0.117	0.219	0.186	0.181	0.155
+ USL-H	0.302	0.304	0.493	0.480	0.551	0.556	0.229	0.237	0.342	0.307	0.185	0.169
+ DEB	0.201	0.217	0.319	0.403	0.463	0.549	**0.345**	**0.325**	0.368	0.391	0.214	0.200
+ DEB + USL-H	0.219	0.270	0.347	0.465	0.484	0.547	0.339	0.311	0.377	**0.395**	0.225	0.215
USL-H	0.322	0.340	0.495	0.523	0.443	0.457	0.108*	0.093*	0.293	0.235	0.217	0.179
+ DEB	0.201	0.269	0.322	0.482	0.452	0.501	0.333	0.258	0.366	0.390	0.224	0.223
All-Metrics	**0.459**	**0.473**	**0.522**	**0.534**	0.566	0.561	0.163	0.149	0.366	0.349	**0.288**	**0.268**

Table 11: Results of different combinations of metrics. All values are statistically significant to $p < 0.05$, unless marked by *. PE is the abbreviation of PredictiveEngage. The last row (All-Metrics), is the average of all the metrics.

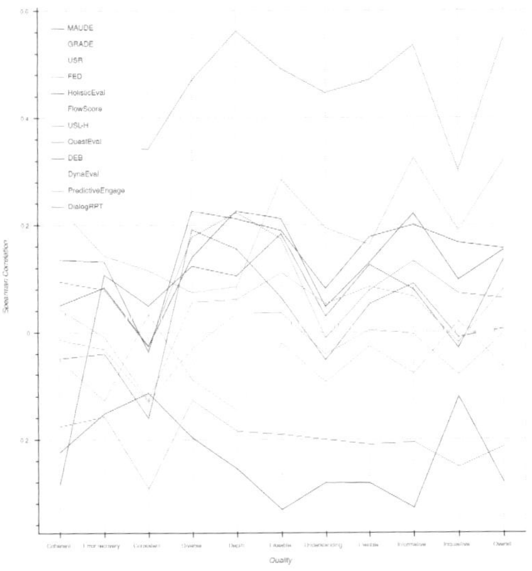

Figure 4: Spearman correlation to dialog-level annotation qualities on the FED data.

C.3 Combining Metrics

Many metrics rely on an ensemble of different models. Inspired by this, this section explores the possibility that a combination of metrics may be successful (Table 11). Since it is not feasible to exhaustively explore all possible combinations of the metrics, some combinations of the best-performing metrics were explored here. The metrics are combined through simple averaging. *Future work should explore more sophisticated mechanisms for combining metrics.*

First, PredictiveEngage, RUBER and PONE were combined, as proposed in (Ghazarian et al., 2020). Indeed, the resulting combined metric shows significant improvement, especially on the USR-TopicalChat and USR-Personachat data, but correlation decreases on other datasets.

Next, combinations of USR, GRADE, USL-H and DEB (the best performing metrics on the referenced quality-annotated datasets) were explored. The combination of USR with GRADE, USL-H, PONE and PredictiveEngage performs better on the USR data as well as on GRADE-ConvAI2. Given the strong performance of GRADE on the GRADE data, combining it with the other metrics negatively impacts its performance. However, combining GRADE and DEB does result in an improvement. Interestingly, combining DEB with USR and USL-H also negatively affects the results. In Figure 3, we observe that the outputs of GRADE and DEB have high correlation to each other, which is an indication of the similar behavior of the two metrics. The output similarities of metrics may be a good indicator for how to best combine metrics.

The last row of Table 11, shows the result of taking the average of the scores of all of the metrics that were assessed in this paper. While the idea of an *All* metric is simple, and metrics are combined through simple averaging, the results are surprisingly good across the different referenced quality annotated datasets. This result highlights the potential of combining various evaluation metrics in some smart manner.